WE DRANK THE WATER

Nazareth in Belize

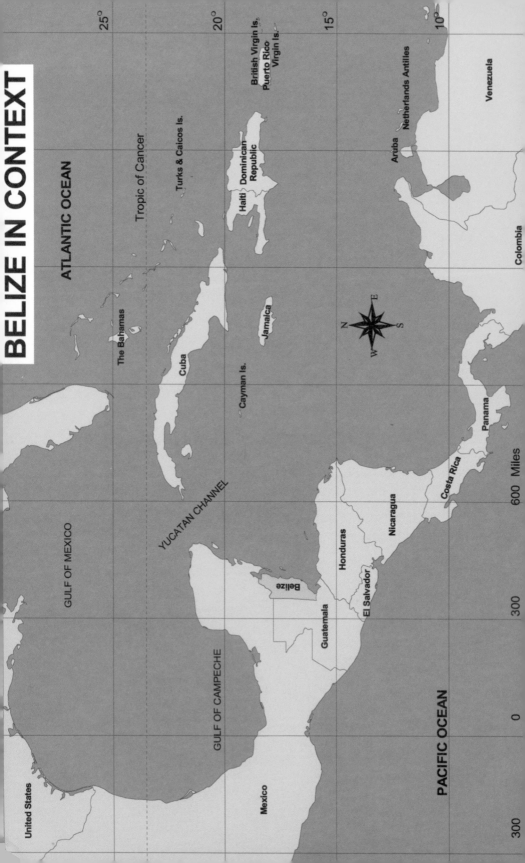

BELIZE IN CONTEXT

WE DRANK THE WATER

Nazareth in Belize

Mary Ransom Burke, SCN

HARMONY HOUSE PUBLISHERS
LOUISVILLE

© 2003 Sisters of Charity of Nazareth
First Edition Printed 2003
by Harmony House Publishers
P.O. Box 90 Prospect Ky. 40059 USA
(502) 228-2010
Production Direction Carol Johnson
(Softbound) ISBN 1-56469-106-3

Printed in Canada

03 02 01 00 99 5 4 3 2 1

Library of congress Cataloging-in-Publication Data

Burke, Mary Ransom, 1911-
    We drank the water : Nazareth in Belize / Mary Ransom Burke.-- 1st ed.

    p. cm.

Includes bibliographical references and index.
    ISBN 1-56469-106-3
    1.   Sisters of Charity of Nazareth (Nazareth,
Ky.)--Missions--Belize--History--20th century.   2.   Missions,
American--Belize--History--20th century.   1.   Title.
    BV2843.B8B87 2003
    2&1'.9107282--dc21
                                    2003006898

*To Mary of Nazareth, emerging quietly into the
new millennium, shed of myth and ancient trappings*

CONTENTS

FOREWORD

Telling the story of the complex land of Belize and its people as experienced by the Sisters of Charity of Nazareth, who began ministering there in 1975, calls for flexibility. Such flexibility is afforded by postmodernism, a writing style that lends itself to combining personal reminiscence with public document—a style that mingles ancient history with history in the making. It allows the author to be in the story and out of it, using memory, reflection, imagination, and research to build an account that explains the precarious yet persistent vision underlying life in a time of growth and speculation. Adapting this style to *We Drank the Water: Nazareth in Belize* has allowed me to intermingle various forms of narrative prose with lyric verse, along with documentation from newspapers, archival records, and memoirs. Shifting from one form to another, I have attempted to recreate the magic and the pain that is this much-loved country, poised with hope at the beginning of the twenty-first century.

Each facet of the Belize story offers a complexity of its own. In the 1970s the SCNs, like most communities of women religious, faced a declining membership at a time when the needs of the world were increasing. How dare they take on a new venture in a land new to them? The Roman Catholic Church, of which the Congregation is a part, was in the throes of renewal initiated by the Second Vatican

Council. How helpful could the Community be in that movement? Belize itself was moving quietly toward independence from Britain. How could the political and religious movements facilitate each other? This foreword offers a simple guide through the pattern of the book. The questions posed from time to time attempt to illuminate the reader's path.

"Why does the beautiful country, Belize, with such fine, capable people need Sisters of Charity of Nazareth—the SCNs?" A similar question might once have been asked about our country of origin. Yet the United States of America has found a need for SCNs for nearly two hundred years. Evidently the answer to both questions lies in the mystery of relationship. No one simply serves. All people everywhere are in service to one another. The manner of service may be as varied as are the flowers of the field, all growing out of the same soil. Ministry of all kinds is love in action growing out of the soil of Divine love, the hope of global survival.Such was the service to which SCNs were called in 1974 when they were asked to assist a pastor in Belize whose parish extended far beyond his reach in both people and miles. The SCN response occurred at the same time that the Lay Ministry Program, officially established at Vatican Council II, was being widely implemented. The response to one parish, then, paved the way to participation in a worldwide movement. That movement brought together scores of people willing, even eager, to serve the Church and one another. In order to serve, preparation was necessary. SCNs participated as both learners and teachers.

In 1974, although our community had served in several countries for many years, SCNs were new to Belize. In accepting ministry there, however, we became part of a diocese in which several congregations of women and men religious had, for a century and more, served the Church generously and courageously. We are honored to have become one of that group. Until 1998 we had lived in whatever place was most convenient to our ministry. In that year, SCN Center

Belize was established and blessed, giving us a sense of being really at home in Belize.

The following pages present Belize as Sisters of Charity of Nazareth have known the country during the last quarter of the twentieth century. Our acquaintance with Belize has grown and developed gradually. To attempt to cast the total narrative in neat historical succession would be to lose the sense of variety that is one of Belize's most valuable qualities. Giving a true picture of the place and the people as well as a comprehensive view of our experience there requires presenting it in episodes.

After the first four chapters, the setting of which is Dangriga in the Stann Creek District, the narrative moves in Chapter Five from Dangriga to San Ignacio in the Cayo District. To attempt to make a transition in the narrative without a description of San Ignacio and its people would be to lose something of the quality that is of the very essence of Belize. Continuity is there and reveals itself as the story moves on. That connection established, Chapter Six continues the Cayo story.

Chapter Seven recounts a visit to Xunantunich, one of Belize's many ancient Maya ruins, where massive structures lend stability to an atmosphere of mystery. A morning there offers an opportunity for quiet reflection before taking up the thread of the story once more in Chapter Eight in Dangriga, this time after the former British colony has become the independent country of Belize.

Chapter Nine takes the reader back to Nazareth, the SCN "Old Kentucky Home," from which two SCNs set out one cold January morning in 1982 for a week-long journey in a Ford truck, their destination Belize City. The City continues to be the scene of the narrative until well into Chapter Fourteen and a period called "A Time of Transition."

Chapter Fifteen moves back in time to 1975 in order to lose nothing of the story of SCNs in the southernmost part of Belize, the Toledo District. That chapter and the one following tell the whole story of SCNs in San Antonio, closing with the year 1993.

Chapter Seventeen begins to recount the story of Independence that opened when San Antonio closed. Chapter Eighteen finds SCNs moving from Independence to Belize City but retaining a bond with Independence by means of regular weekend visits with strong development and support of lay ministry there.

Chapter Nineteen features Maya Center, one of the villages associated with Independence, and one that the family of SCN Mary Lynn Fields has assisted through support of Hermelindo Saqui, a Mayan lay missionary.

Chapter Twenty opens with the blessing of the SCN Center in Belize City, continues with the celebration of our twenty-fifth anniversary in the country in the year 2000, and concludes with the participation that same year of an SCNAssociate in a special session of the United Nations.

To follow the Lay Ministry Program in Belize from its official beginning in 1975 to the participation of one of the lay ministers in a special session held at the UN in the year 2000 is to share twenty-five years of joys and sorrows, hopes fulfilled and hopes left unsatisfied. These pages will show that the accomplishments of those twenty-five years were built upon a firm foundation of more than a century of service by the Church, especially by the several religious congregations that have served and that continue to serve with the people of Belize.

Few of us realize how far we have come in our thinking as we have experienced some of the results of Vatican Council II, which opened October 11, 1962, and closed December 8, 1964. While incalculable change remains to be effected, and while there is need of awareness of the tendency to slip back into pre-Vatican habits, the change that has been implemented is bearing fruit abundantly. Fortunately, the Lay Ministry Program is one of the fruit-bearing enactments. Much remains to be done, but, as these pages will demonstrate, the basic movement is firm, and its implementation in Belize is strong.

ACKNOWLEDGMENTS

How does one acknowledge the countless items, large and small, that contribute to the creation of a volume like this that involves countless people, places, and periods of time? The answer, of course, is that it is impossible to do it comprehensively. The best one can do is to try.

The seed of *We Drank the Water* was planted by SCN Barbara Thomas, President of the Congregation a number of years ago, at a time when a Belizean event was being celebrated at Nazareth. Barbara asked several of us who had been in ministry in Belize to write some recollections of our experience there. We did that, each one contributing her bit to SCN history in Belize. I recall remarking at the time how inadequate bits like that really are. In response I was encouraged to tell the broader story. It was not a definite assignment, so I didn't begin right away. When, however, more and more people who had not been to Belize began to ask questions about that little Caribbean country, I felt an urge to proceed.

I am grateful for the encouragement that I have received from the Congregation through SCNs Bridgid Clifford and Mary Elizabeth Miller, successively Vice President for Stewardship and Planning, from Patricia Worley, SCN, and the other coordinators of Russell Hall, and from many SCNs and SCNAs who continue to manifest interest in spite of my delays in publication. I appreciate the willingness of some who, having spent several years in Belize, were willing to read some very rough copy and give very valuable criticism. Then I appreciate members of my family and friends who have called my attention to the ever-growing information about Belize in the press.

One special resource of importance to anyone planning to publish is excellent proofreaders. I have been so fortunate as to find three—two who can spot a superfluous comma as well as the absence of a necessary one, and one who questions whole statements, sending the writer back to sources for validation. SCNs Irene Satory and Rachel Willett qualify as the former, SCN Rosemarie Kirwan, with long Belizean experience, as the latter. Following those resources, our official SCN editors Mary Collette Crone and Lucy Marie Freibert, assisted by SCNs Margaret Maria Coon and Margaret Rodericks, ready every SCN publication for the printer. Lucy and Mary Collette have contributed far beyond the call of duty. Then, too, I would like to acknowledge our faithful and gracious courier, SCN Regina Atkins.

In my many years as a teacher of English and as an SCN journalist, I had never written a book. If I thought that the latter would be simply more extensive and intensive journalistic writing, I was wrong. I took sole responsibility for scores of news stories, some of which have proved helpful references in this present enterprise. Those stories and much more valuable information have been available because of Nazareth's excellent archives—archivist SCN Bridgid Clifford and her staff, especially SCNs Margaret Maria and Anna Catherine Coon.

When writing a book, an author's expression of appreciation often includes schools and universities that nurtured intellectual growth, and rightly so. I do appreciate every day of my formal education. Education begins, however, long before the dawn of school days. My father introduced me to Shakespeare before I had completed the first grade. Dad's accounts of the theatre were based on his boyhood experience as a stagehand at old Macauley's Theatre in Louisville. He and his friends had earned seats in the balcony by doing chores backstage and creating sound effects in the days when Louisville was at the top of the theatre ladder. His love of theatre and books influenced me greatly.

My interest in writing was further developed by my mother, who kept me busy writing stories during a siege of diphtheria when I was eight. The epidemic was serious. Children I knew died of it, and doctors were keeping patients in bed. While ill, I wrote a "novel" and was broken-hearted at having to let it be burned because "it was filled with germs." Mother assured me that that was just a practice book and that there would be others.

The manuscript of this kind of book would be far from adequate without accompanying photographs, each one of which is worth the proverbial thousand words. I wish I might supply the name of each photographer. The best I can do is to credit those veteran SCN missionaries who were wise enough to collect and keep some very good shots that not only reflect the text but truly enrich it. The photographs shared here are, for the most part, from the collections of SCNs Sarah Ferriell, Ann Kernen, Rosemarie Kirwan, John Loretto Mueller, Judy Raley, SCNA Trudi Maish, and the Office of Congregational Advancement.

Maps provide a sense of relatedness of parts of a country to each other and a country's place within a hemispheric context. For the maps provided herein, I am grateful to Joseph G. Harrington and Robert W. Forbes of the University of Louisville Center for GIS, Department of Geography and Geosciences.

Today, it is a rare publication that does not utilize a computer in the composition process. Thanks to the former SCN Louisville Regional Betty Blandford, I had the use of a computer from the beginning of the process. At first I used it in a cubicle at Spalding University library, by courtesy of the librarian. The resources of that library have been a lifelong source of enrichment. The computer accompanied me to Nazareth, where the Telecommunications Department, coordinated by Anthony Garvey, ably assisted by Jennifer Hughes and Mary Martin, has not only kept it in tiptop condition but has also consistently improved its capacity.

When, in September 2000, we celebrated in Belize twenty-five years spent in that country, I had the opportunity to visit the comparatively new Belize Public Library. Two reference librarians there were most helpful with the research on special events, such as the celebration of Belizean Independence and Pope John Paul's visit there. It is also a joy to recall that an e-mail from SCNs in India assured the Sisters in Belize that, as the celebration occurred in Central America, a similar one took place in Mokama, thanking God for SCNs' twenty-five years in Belize.

Finally, every publication worthy of the name must have a cover, and the cover should be authentic, artistic, and attractive. I approached SCN Luke Boiarski because she is an authentic, accomplished artist. She agreed to be responsible for the cover rather than to do it herself, explaining that printing today, with its sophisticated technology, utilizes more than the gifts of the artist. We agreed to that so long as Luke supervised the creation of the cover. After negotiating with graphic designer Jerry Farmer and sharing our interest in having some semblance of the Forty Foot Falls and the toucan— Belize's national bird—we have, as you see, a veritable taste of Belize.

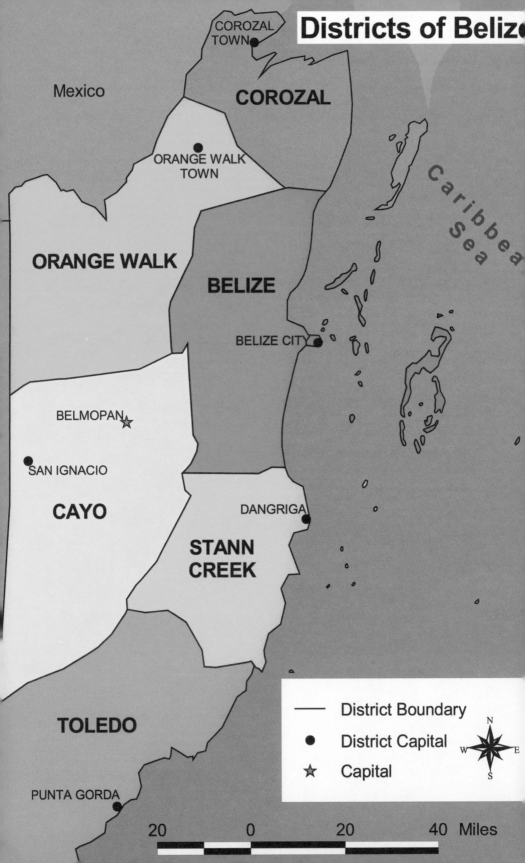

Chapter One

A LEGEND AND A LEGACY

"Drink the water of Belize and you'll surely come back." So runs a legend among the people of that country just south of the Yucatan Peninsula. The source of the legend, like much of the history of the land, is unrecorded, but the truth of it is proved day after day. Ask many a visitor, "How many times have you been to Belize?" The answer may well be, "I have lost count. I come every chance I get." Carlos Ledson Miller's recent novel, *Belize*, carries the legend in the author's note following the table of contents. I had hoped that he might have named the source of the legend, but he simply calls the legend a Belizean proverb. During the twenty-five years' presence of the Sisters of Charity of Nazareth in that country, more than a hundred members of the Congregation and their Associates have either visited or been in ministry there, some of them more than once.

Water is never far away in Belize. In addition to the Caribbean Sea, which forms its eastern boundary, there are countless rivers and lakes with little streams branching off from them here and there. One of those streams, the North Stann Creek River, flows through the town of Dangriga from west to east. Among the trees growing along its banks is the gumaga, or provision tree, somewhat like the mango tree. The neighborhood nearby, following Belizean custom, is called Gumagarugu, *rugu* meaning surrounding area.

The SCNs' first acquaintance with Belize, as the following chapters reveal, was in Dangriga. When I wanted to get in touch with our early experience in Belize, then, Dangriga was the logical place to go. Although a part of Central America, Belize is better known as a Caribbean country.

The official language of Belize is English, but Spanish has long been prominent in the northern and western districts that border on Mexico and Guatemala respectively. In recent years, refugees from Guatemala, El Salvador, and Honduras have been coming to Belize in great numbers, causing Spanish to be heard more frequently. English and Spanish are not the only languages spoken in Belize, however. About one third of the people of Belize are Creole (descendants of Africans), according to Mahler and Wotkyns in *Belize, a Natural Destination,* p. 31. For private conversation, they have developed and use a Creole English that most of the people of Belize have adopted and regularly use for convenience.

Of the many different ethnic groups in the country, the one with the oldest history is Indian. The beginning of Indian history in Belize is lost in antiquity, but the presence of numerous Maya ruins, some dating to pre-Christian times, is a constant reminder that the Indians were there in great numbers. Those there now, however, forming about eight percent of the population, are considered by many historians not to be direct descendants of those who left remnants of their ancient presence. According to that theory, the prehistoric people left in self-defense or were driven out. Evidence suggests that each Indian city-state was so independent that when one was attacked from without there was not sufficient unity among the various groups within to withstand the onslaught.

The current Indian population in Belize consists of Maya, Maya-Mopan, and Ketchi, who speak their respective languages, along with English. The Maya came from Mexico and Guatemala in mid nineteenth century to escape the War of the Castes—a war in Yucatan that continued from 1847 to 1857 in protest against the caste system that had developed under the Spanish. About 1886

Maya-Mopan came from Guatemala to escape forced labor and taxation. At approximately the same time, Ketchi from Guatemala came to Belize to escape "their virtual enslavement by German coffee growers." Belief persists, however, that some of the ancient Maya never left Belize and that, therefore, some of the present Maya are their direct descendants, as Assad Shoman asserts in *Thirteen Chapters of a History of Belize,* p. 5. Artifacts found in the massive ruins of that ancient civilization indicate that the Indian people of Central America were highly intelligent and accomplished. In *Inside Belize,* p. 77, Tom Barry writes: "The Mayas' discovery of the concept of zero, the base of modern arithmetic, and their comprehension of the mysteries of time are testaments of the advanced character of their civilization."

Gumagarugu, through which flows the North Stann Creek River, is a part of Dangriga in the Stann Creek District, one of the country's six geographic and political sections. Many of the people who live in the area, as well as in numerous other places in Belize and in the United States, are Garifuna. They speak English, but they have preserved the language of their African and Carib Indian heritage along with many other characteristics of that culture.

So well have the Garifuna people preserved their heritage that in 1998 the Field Museum in Chicago held a three-day conference on the Garifuna culture, explaining that they chose that culture because it offers rich grounds for research. Barbara Flores, SCN, who is Garifuna and who was in doctoral studies at Garrett School of Theology and Northwestern University at that time, was one of the presenters in the Field Museum program.

Relationship between the Garifuna and the Sisters of Charity of Nazareth began in 1974, when SCNs Mary Lynn Fields and Susan Gatz spent the summer in Dangriga. Now the relationship extends far beyond the original Garifuna/SCN connection. Belizeans who are SCNs, or who are becoming SCNs, include persons of Lebanese, Hispanic, Maya Indian, and Creole background. Amina Bejos, SCN, for example, who currently teaches at Lexington Catholic High

School in Lexington, Kentucky, is from the Cayo District of Belize, where frequently the Spanish language is heard and many Spanish customs are practiced. Her name—Amina—reflects also some Lebanese ancestry. Higinia Bol, SCN, from the Toledo District, is of a Maya-Mopan family.

Because the North Stann Creek River flows from west to east through the center of Dangriga, the main bridge of the town is the scene of a constant stream of people of various ethnic groups on foot, on bikes, in cars, trucks, and buses. I hold that I am not superstitious, but I have to admit that, even as I write at a distance of a thousand miles, the magnetism of that scene draws me back. Yes, while I lived there I drank the water, and I have returned to Belize many times.

During one of those visits, I stood one afternoon beside the busy road near the river, aware of multiple activities but not really seeing them. I was absorbed in my own troubled thoughts, thoughts I would have to share with Maggie, my term of endearment for Gumagarugu.

"Maggie," I said, "you're no help. You entice me here to write about this beautiful country that I love, then you stand there peacefully, your leaves shimmering in the sunlight, leaving me with pages that read like a commercial tour book. I refuse to stand here watching you ignore my plight."

I closed my eyes in defiance of her peacefulness and stood there, gradually becoming conscious of the life around me. Soon I was experiencing the sounds of Belize, the rumble of trucks, the steady flow of voices punctuated now and then by shrill laughter of children, the cry of hawks above, the swish of waves in the distance, and the lap of the water against the small boats along the banks of the river, the very pulse of Belize.

Maggie, in spite of my defiance, was responding. She seemed to be saying, "If you really love Belize, write from your heart. Break through your objective, journalistic style. Belize is alive; she will breathe life into every word you write."

A chorus of giggles startled me out of my reverie. I opened my eyes and found a group of five little girls staring up at me. As they turned and ran, I heard one of them say, "She not correct." "So," I thought, "not correct. Well, maybe one does have to be a little mad to think that she can convey through the written word some semblance of this gem of a country."

The little girls were just about to turn right at the next bend in the road when one of them came skipping back to me. She took my hand and held it, fascinated by the contrast between her plump dark brown and my skinny sunburned white. Standing on one foot, swinging the other, and still holding my hand, she looked up at me with her soft, brown eyes.

"Where are your friends?" I asked. She giggled and pointed to the little group peeping around the corner of a house down the road. Then I realized that they had probably dared her to approach this woman who was "not correct."

"You go to school?" I asked, searching for some way to engage this six-year-old in conversation. After indicating "yes" by deep bows of the head, she held firmly to my hand and looked up quizzically with her large, brown eyes. For a moment there was a silent exchange of understanding between us, but the voices of her friends, screaming, "Come on, come on, come on," brought the encounter to a close.

I don't even know her name. Learning it would have been a better opener than the question I asked, but a conversation was not to be. The little girl had taken a dare. She had proved to her friends that she was brave enough to approach a woman who was "not correct," as the Belizeans put it, even to hold her hand. As is frequently the case, the stouthearted proved to be warmhearted as well.

The encounter might have taken place anywhere in the world, but the memory that I have of it is authentically Belizean. It is like a painting by a consummate artist: the river flowing into the sea, the big shrimp boats out there, the small fishing boats beside the dusty road, the crowds passing by, the little girls peeping around the corner of the house, my little friend torn between loyalty to her peers and the attraction of a new experience with someone who looks so different yet whose manner assures her that, given time, they could become friends.

That incident epitomizes my relationship with Belize. Belize is for me, not only a Caribbean country south of Mexico, not only a multiethnic people with a history, not only a land with history hidden in its soil. It is all of these, but it is more, much, much more.

So, with Maggie's advice nudging me on, and with a need to share with those who have not "drunk the water" the priceless experience that awaits them, I move on to another Belizean treasure, the Cockscomb Basin Wildlife Sanctuary, also in the Stann Creek District.

Mark Nolan of the World Wildlife Fund, quoted on the back cover of *Cockscomb Basin Wildlife Sanctuary,* has called the sanctuary a "magical place where wonders and diversity are accessible to both the casual and the serious visitor." And he adds, "A visit to the Basin is invigorating to the human spirit; it engenders a harmony with nature." Many others have come under this spell. In the "Foreword" to the valuable study, Alan Rabinowitz of the Wildlife Conservation Society of New York, who spent several years in the Sanctuary studying the jaguar, writes:

> In the years that have followed since I left Belize, I have worked and traveled in many parts of the world. But I can never remember more than a month going by that I did not reflect back on the people, the animals, and the mystique of the Cockscomb Basin. (p. xi)

Commenting on the "increasing strident cry" against closing areas such as the Cockscomb as parks and sanctuaries because of the increasing human population, Rabinowitz recalls:

> When I initiated efforts to protect the Cockscomb Basin, it was not for jaguars alone that I labored. I had already seen how the destruction of habitat and the unsustainable use of forest

resources was decimating many of the wild areas of Belize and was leaving the forests around many local villages quiet and empty. I believed in my heart that if we could protect the Cockscomb, the local people and all Belizeans would realize what treasure they had saved. The truth is that I never expected such a change in thinking to occur as quickly as it has. My admiration goes out to the local Mayan communities around the Cockscomb Basin Wildlife Sanctuary and to the Belizean people as a whole for their foresight and commitment. (p. xii)

Rabinowitz goes on to congratulate the authors and illustrators of the book, calling it a "valuable addition to the natural history literature of Belize and the Central American Region." Then, realizing that none of this could have been done without government approval, he expresses "heartfelt thanks to the Government of Belize and to all those Mayan families who have helped give Cockscomb to the future generations of the world" (p. xii).

I experienced the harmony of the Sanctuary in an unusual way when I visited there with friends one day in the late nineties. That day in the lodge at the Basin, I asked our party to go on without me to investigate jaguars. It was no lack of interest in jaguars that detained me, but a series of display boards in the lodge that promised to answer a question that had long been tantalizing me: *How did Belize come to be?* This second smallest country on the American continent, with the Caribbean Sea as its eastern border, comprises within its 8,886 square miles a mountain range that includes a peak of 3,699 feet, a waterfall of 1,000 feet, the second longest coral reef in the world, as well as numerous rivers and lakes. Traveling from the northernmost to the southernmost tip of the country means covering only 174 miles; from eastern coast to western border at the widest point only sixty-three miles. Yet, traveling in any direction one is surrounded by 700 varieties of orchids, 533 species of birds, 155 species of mammals, 107 species of reptiles.

The population of Belize, while numbering fewer than 300,000, includes seven different ethnic groups: Creole, Mestizo, Garifuna,

Maya-Mopan and Ketchi, Chinese, American (USA), and German, the latter chiefly members of the Mennonite Community.

Good bulletin boards have a way not only of displaying history and other information but also of moving observers to pursue the information for themselves. Those display boards were of the latter kind. I asked them to be my graphic tour guide. They responded immediately, taking me at once to the dawn of creation. I had been there previously through reading of the big bang or listening to lectures about it, but those experiences had left me wandering in a maze of gigantic rocks for billions of years.

The display before me, by focusing on Belize's place in creation history, made the otherwise bewildering aspect of the evolutionary process easy to grasp. The first board summarizes the early movements of the universe, suggesting that over millions of years the movement would necessarily have caused great geological changes, such as the breaking up of the earth's crust into what we now call continents.

The second board takes the viewer to a period about 350 million years ago when, as many geologists believe, North America was connected with Greenland, Northern Europe, and Russia, forming Laurasia. At that time, Belize is supposed to have been completely covered by ocean. There were no trees or mountains, only layers of sediment slowly accumulating on the ocean floor.

One hundred million years later, the sediment on the ocean floor was crushed between colliding plates of earth. The force of the collision was so intense that huge blocks of the sea floor crumbled under the pressure and were forced upward along two fault lines to form a mighty mountain range that we now know as the Maya Mountains.

Continuing to follow the directions of my newly found graphic guide, I tried to adjust my imagination to a period of about 200 million years ago when molten magma from deep within the earth melted up toward the earth's surface. If the magma had escaped through a crack in the earth's crust, I am reminded, it would have erupted as a volcano. Instead, the magma was trapped below the earth's surface where it cooled to form granite. This massive intrusion, so different from the surrounding rock, formed, at the same time, mountains and level land that we call Mountain Pine Ridge and the Hummingbird Mullins area, respectively.

Then about 100 million years ago the sea began to rise, covering all but the highest peaks of what are now Maya Mountains. *What is now Belize was an island.* In the deep sea, thick layers of limestone were deposited. Later, the sea dropped and the limestone was exposed. In many places, the soft limestone, later dissolved by the force of rivers and streams, formed caves, sinkholes, and underground streams. At the same time, faulting action caused chunks of sea floor to drop, creating ridges in the shallow sea. This action formed bases for Belize's offshore atolls and eventually the famous barrier reef. Mere theory? Theory, perhaps, but plausible, and the Maya Mountains, the *atolls,* and the *barrier reef* present a pretty substantial Exhibit A. (An atoll is a ring-shaped coral reef, or a string of closely spaced small coral islands enclosing or nearly encircling a shallow lagoon.)

Then, in April 2000, Exhibit B was published. *National Geographic* carried that month (pp. 54-71) an amazing story of the current exploration of Central America's longest cave: "On a recent expedition cavers mapped a vital link in this labyrinth of four huge caves carved through limestone in Belize and Guatemala by rainwater and the subterranean Chiquibul River" (p. 55). Lead researcher Thomas Miller says, "Explorers have mapped some 40 convoluted miles and suspect another 20 are yet to be found" (p. 61).

Why was the creation process so exceedingly generous to Belize? Is it merely the way things worked out, or was there some special divine plan? Whatever the reason, many people have enjoyed the beauty of the country as well as the benefits of its fruits. Many people, likewise, have contributed to its development and many continue to do so.

For more than a century, Belize was a colony of Britain, becoming independent September 21, 1981. Britain encouraged and facilitated the education of the children of Belize, but generally the country experienced the effects of colonialism.

As would be expected, the recent history of religion and education in Belize begins with the Anglican Church, the Church of England. That Church made a good beginning in the country. St. John's Cathedral in Belize City is the oldest cathedral in Central America (1826). A second Anglican church in Belize City, St. Mary's, has a large parish and school there today. Narda Dobson, in *A History of Belize*, p. 160, points out, however, that by 1856 there were in Belize City 240 Presbyterians, 500 Baptists, 500 Wesleyans, 1,000 Roman Catholics, 2,500 members of the Church of England, and 2,600 others. Although Dobson does not identify those "others," many of them were probably Mayan or Ketchi, who frequently maintained their native manner of worship.

It was the Caste Wars of the Yucatan that brought Mexicans down to Belize, and it was they who sought to follow the Roman Catholic faith they knew. At first, in about 1851, a few Jesuits came from England and other European countries to serve them, but finally the needs proved greater than the numbers available could handle. In 1893, therefore, they turned over the Belize mission to the Jesuits of the St. Louis Province in the United States (Dobson, p. 319). Jesuits from that province, together with the Benedictines and the diocesan clergy, currently serve Belize.

Several other religious communities have served Belize for many years. The Sisters of Mercy celebrated their centenary in Belize more than a decade ago, the Sisters of the Holy Family in 1998. The Pallottine Sisters have served there since 1913. Those who have come more recently are the Benedictine priests and brothers and the Sisters of Charity of Nazareth. The Benedictines celebrated twenty-five years in Belize in 1996, the Sisters of Charity of Nazareth in the year 2000. Each group has its own story. Some stories are similar, but no two are identical. Together they reflect the manner in which, through

God's call, the charisms of many are blended to meet the multiple needs of a people.

The SCN story began with a prelude in 1974, when SCNs Mary Lynn Fields and Susan Gatz spent the summer in Belize. Mary Lynn was responding to the request of Barbara Thomas, SCN, President of the Congregation, that she consider ministry there. Lynn asked Susan to accompany her for companionship and for possible need of a translator, should Spanish predominate among any group of people in the country. (Lynn, as she was known generally in Belize, is sometimes referred to as Mary Lynn, as she was called by her family and by many SCNs.)

Susan recalls:

> It was a relaxed and grace-filled summer. We learned to love the slower pace as we adjusted ourselves to the rhythm of life in a tropical country. We had many mind- and heart-expanding experiences. We savored new foods, enjoyed the lushness of the jungle plants and lived with a new-found—and life altering—simplicity. Above all, we learned to love the people of Belize who welcomed us into their homes and shared with us their families, customs, and faith.

Susan recalls too that, as they relaxed in the afternoons, Lynn was reading, with deep interest, Gustavo Gutierrez's *Theology of Liberation*.

At the end of that summer, Lynn and Susan returned to the States, but both of them "had drunk the water of Belize." Susan took up ministry in the States; several years later she became Provincial of the Southern Province, of which Belize was a part, a position that required her to visit there periodically.

Lynn returned to Memphis Catholic High School in Tennessee, where she had been missioned previously and where she would continue as a member of the faculty for another year. At the end of that year, in response to the call of the Community, she went to the new mission in Dangriga in the Stann Creek District of Belize. In order that she might not be alone in the house that the parish provided for her, a Sister of Mercy, Marian Joseph Baird, from St. Catherine Academy joined her. Later, Lynn was joined also by SCNs Anna Marie Nalley, Kitty Wilson, and later still by Patricia Kelley, SCN, who had recently returned from twenty-five years in India. It was, therefore, in September of 1975 that the Sisters of Charity of Nazareth became a part of the Church's mission to Belize in Central America.

Although a part of Central America, Belize is better known as a Caribbean country.

Belize

Mexico

Guatemala

Caribbean Sea

San Andres
Xaibe
Patchakan
Paraiso
COROZAL TOWN
Cristo Rey
Conceptione
Louisville
Ranchito
Calcutta
Sarteneja
San Narciso
Santa Clara
Cunox
San Joaquin
San Victor
San Pablo
Libertad
Progresso
San Jose
Little Belize
Yo Creek
Caledonia
San Lazaro
San Estevan
Trinidad
ORANGE WALK TOWN
August Pine Ridge
Trial Farm
San Jose Palmar
San Filipe
Guinea Grass
Maskall
Shipyard
Blue Creek
Crooked Tree

Sand Hill
Lqadyville
Burrell Boom
Double Head Cabbage
Valley of Peace Big Falls
Santa Familia
Hattieville
BELIZE CITY
Spanish Lookout
Roaring Creek
Bullet Tree Falls
BELMOPAN
Teakettle
Salvapan
Las Flores
Camalote
Unitedville
Alta Vista
Central Farm
Esperanza
Pomona
SAN IGNACIO
DANGRIGA
San Jose Succotz
Silk Grass
Benque Viejo Del Carmen
Hopkins
Red Bank
Maya Center
Maya Mopan
Georgetown
Indepependence
Seine Bight
Mango Creek
Placencia
Cow Pen
Big Creek
San Jose
San Antonio
San Pedro Columbia
Pueblo Viejo
Jalacte
PUNTA GORDA
Dolores
Cirque Sarco

Legend

- City
- District Capital
- Nation Capital
- Roads
- Rivers
- Maya Mountains

N
W — E
S

20   0   20   40 Miles

Chapter Two

DANGRIGA:
A CLOSER VIEW

Twenty-five years of independence have brought about startling changes in Belize—startling changes, but not sweeping ones. To go north across the bridge over the North Stann Creek River in Dangriga is to experience both stability and expansion. The vehicular section now easily accommodates two-way traffic, and the sturdy walls separating the vehicular traffic from pedestrians ensure safety, especially for the scores of children who skip and run across the bridge all day long.

Across the bridge, however, Commerce Street is much the same as it was in the summer of 1974 when SCNs Mary Lynn Fields and Susan Gatz responded to the invitation to serve the Church in Belize temporarily. In 2002 there are more cars and buses and, perhaps, more people. Of the series of shops that line the street on either side, however, many have been there for a generation or more. It is possible to buy clothes or furniture or food or hardware or stationery or almost anything there. It just takes time and practice to learn where to find particular items.

To stay with the river for a while, before further exploration of Commerce Street, one must turn right immediately after crossing the bridge. There, set up along the northern bank of the river as it flows eastward to the sea, is a series of temporary booths tended by shopkeepers from Mexico. The men who set up the shops bring in their merchandise each morning at daybreak and cart home every evening whatever they have not sold. Those short, stocky men have their own methods. They carry exceedingly heavy loads on their backs or push carts that are neatly packed but stretched far beyond reasonable capacity.

Dangriga's cordiality toward shopkeepers from their neighboring country to the north is indicative of the good relationship that has existed for a long time between Belize and Mexico. That relationship is much stronger than Belize's relationship with its Central-American neighbors, even though Belize is itself a Central-American country.

The "river road" leads to Dangriga's market, where a plentiful supply of a limited variety of fruits and vegetables, as well as staples and some meats, is available early in the day. If the many wise, industrious housewives have preceded the visitor to the market, few choices remain.

The market is at the corner where sea and river meet. Proceeding north on Front Street, the visitor passes the Town Hall, the local government offices, the Anglican church, a ballpark surrounded by high fences, a few homes, and a doctor's office. The Caribbean shoreline slopes gradually westward at Dangriga so that Commerce Street, which we left at the bridge, and Front Street, each seeming to maintain apparent straightforward direction ahead, actually meet at Tenth Street. Shortly before the point of meeting are located the large compound of Sacred Heart Church and School and the convent of the Holy Family Sisters, who have staffed the school for more than a century.

Dangriga is the central town of the Stann Creek District, one of the six official districts of the country. The population of 6,600 is mostly Garifuna and Creole. It is challenging to walk along Front Street after the early morning Mass, joining the large group of women who, having begun the day with Mass at Sacred Heart Church, are now going home to take up the day's work. These women welcome anyone who joins them, hardly aware that the visitor does not understand Garifuna. Their fluency in the language belies the fact that for many years educators discouraged its use. To be part of the life of the members of that group even briefly, however, is to experience something of their energy and kindly purposefulness, even when one does not understand the conversation. They move on to their homes, many nearby, others across a bridge to the south where Commerce Street becomes St. Vincent Street, named for the island from which many early settlers came. There, right on the sea, south of Havana Creek, stands Holy Ghost School, built to catch the overflow from Sacred Heart School and now itself overflowing.

Dangriga is growing in many directions. In the north, ten streets branch westward from Benguche Avenue immediately past the old cemetery where occasional ceremonies keep departed loved ones ever in mind. On St. Vincent Street at the south end are some commercial enterprises, but not the numerous shops observed on Commerce Street. About fifty miles from Dangriga along the Hummingbird Highway is Belmopan, the present capital of the country. Belize City, the former capital, is 105 miles distant.

The change in location of the capital occurred when a hurricane nearly wiped Belize City off the map in October 1961. Only thirty years earlier, Britain had rebuilt that capital city, of what was then its colony, after an even more devastating hurricane. Belize City is situated on the Caribbean Sea; therefore, it is especially vulnerable to storms. It was Britain's decision to establish the new inland capital city, calling it Belmopan, Bel for Belize and Mopan for Maya-Mopan, the earliest known occupants of the land. The change in location of the capital had little effect on Dangriga, but it cut the distance to the capital in half. It remained necessary, however, to make many trips to Belize City, for at first, only the government agencies moved to the new capital; many other places of business did not move.

Britain had been concerned about the vulnerability of the location of a capital city on the sea, and rightly so. The sea, nevertheless, has an attraction for nearly everyone who is so fortunate as to see it in all its splendor—its threatening harshness, its sparkling brightness, its foreboding grayness, its rippling peacefulness at sunrise and sunset. The Caribbean Sea itself tends to be especially calm along the shore of Belize most of the time because the coral reef ordinarily breaks the force of the waves.

Although memories of the Garifuna people bring to mind immediately the town of Dangriga, the Garifuna are not limited to that town, nor to the Stann Creek District, nor even to the country of Belize. Because there is a large Garifuna community in Dangriga, however, the national celebration of Garifuna Settlement Day, November 19, is centered there. That celebration recalls the November day in 1823 when a large group of wandering Garifuna joined together with a group already established in Dangriga and made their home there.

Garifuna history begins much earlier, however, when a ship carrying men from Africa, to be sold into slavery, was shipwrecked off the islands of Dominica and St. Vincent. The Africans escaped to the islands and intermingled with the aboriginal Arawak women. History and observation of the families that descended from that union reveal a people with a knowledge of their background, who continue customs and rituals inherited from their ancestors. As a people, they remained free and independent for a number of years. They were finally overcome by the British, however, and driven to the islands off Honduras.

For a generation many Garifuna wandered up and down the coast of Central America, making occasional settlements in Belize, Guatemala, Costa Rica, Nicaragua, and Honduras. Their survival as a people and their ability to maintain much of their original culture wherever they went attest to their strength. An event recounted in the Jesuit publication, *Belizean Studies* (Vol. I, No. 6), reveals some of those characteristics.

Having been driven off the island of St. Vincent, the Africans moved toward Honduras, occupied at that time by the Spanish. The latter were alarmed by what they considered to be an attack by "thousands of Caribs," and forces were sent to repel them. The Garifuna, however, proved to be "quite friendly." The Spanish commander, therefore, "consulted again with his government," and "the Caribs were finally invited to come to the mainland." More than a century later, the Garifuna continue to maintain their culture and manifest their strength. For example, in New York City, where there are a number of Garifuna, their language is one of those recognized by the public school system.

Tom Barry, *Inside Belize,* p. 74, points out that Garifuna are both fishermen and farmers, as well as "exceptional students and linguists, . . . teachers and civil servants." It is not surprising, then, that annually November 19 and the week leading up to that date offer a wealth of opportunities to observe, even to join in, music and dancing, prayer and art, drama and general camaraderie. Variety characterizes the music of Belize. Accompaniment to the many dancers and mimes is often impromptu. Bands, orchestras, and soloists of numerous styles abound.

Anyone who has lived in Belize, not only in Dangriga, can attest to having heard for weeks before Settlement Day the distant sound of early morning drumming practice. Many people hearing it morning after morning wonder why so much practice is necessary, for to them it sounds all right the first time. No one complains, however, and everyone looks forward to the very general revelry on the day itself. Tom Barry substantiates what many of us have experienced. On that day St. Vincent Street is closed in order that it may be given over to the dancers, singers, and providers of refreshment, to the revelers generally. Similar celebrations take place on Christmas Eve, at which time a character known as John Canoe, or Kanu, is prominent. A kind of trickster, Canoe is a clownish figure with a painted face. He wears a mask and a costume of many colors, and begs for rum, candy, or money. He is carrying on a tradition that dates back to slavery days, as his occasional imitation of a slave master reveals to those who can interpret his actions. Here and there someone

John Canoe/Kanu

from the crowd responds to his pleas, tossing him change and candy. If anyone supplies rum, it is not done publicly. Children often run along beside him, hoping to share in the fruits of his performance.

Within the last decade, a specifically indigenous music has developed and has spread far and wide. Garifuna women sing an old song and response as they make cassava bread, a two-day process that requires grinding of cassava root, careful processing, mixing of ingredients, and baking. Recently, rock bands have recognized the value of the song for their own use. When Andy Palacio and Pen

Garifuna women sing an old song and response as they make cassava bread, a two-day process, that requires grinding of cassava root, careful processing, and baking. Here a Garifuna woman engages in one stage of the process.

Cayetano adopted it for their bands, it became known as Punta Rock, and its popularity spread, first countrywide, now world wide. T-shirts proclaiming "Punta till you drop" gave unsolicited advertisement to this distinctively Belizean rock. Barry points out that "punta rock carries a message of cultural consciousness." He quotes the words of one of the songs, *"Uwalla, Uwalla, Uwalla Busingano"* ("Let's be proud, have no shame.").

Although Britain saw to it that the children of British Honduras (the old name of Belize) learned the basics, there was little or no education in the arts. Many gifted Belizeans, however, found ways of expressing those gifts. The Garifuna gift of craftmaking, for example, is demonstrated in the carving of musical instruments, and various styles of art can be found in shops, homes, and public buildings. Some artists use as inspiration the old folk style demonstrated in the celebrations of Settlement Day. Of the fifteen shops in Belize recommended by the critics, two are in Dangriga—Melinda's Historical

Museum and the shop of artist Benjamin Nicholas. Nicholas's paint-
ings are seen in many prominent places throughout the country; he
is also very well known abroad.

Dangriga's gift of celebrating in art, music, and dance is matched
by other accomplishments in the Stann Creek District where Dangriga is located. One of those is the raising of bananas, mangos,
pineapples, as well as oranges and other citrus fruits in Big Creek,
Independence, and Mango Creek, villages just off the Southern Highway. The road through Stann Creek Valley is a lane through citrus
land. At certain seasons—several each year—travelers standing on
trucks can reach up to pluck an orange or two in passing. People
accustomed to getting their oranges in the supermarket cringe to see
fruit that has dropped to the road being crushed by the passing
trucks. Despite that loss, however, workers gather in most of the citrus, much of which is converted to juice to be exported.

Even as the orange groves disappear from sight in the rear view
mirror, the experienced traveler in the valley knows that banana
plantations are nearby. Seeing them may require turning down side
roads, but the experience is well worth the detour. A banana plantation does not offer the aesthetic pleasure of an orange grove, especially when it is necessary to wrap the stalks in treated casings in
order to prevent the blights that can ruin a whole season's crop.
Blights have been known to be so serious and so frequent as to cause
plantations to be completely abandoned. Wrapped or unwrapped,
however, row upon row of stalks of bananas is an impressive sight.
Not long ago, a small group of workers would have attached several
stalks to a bamboo pole and transported them on their shoulders to
a large tent-like enclosure where they would have been sorted,
washed, and packed for shipping. Today, hooks and cables make the
work easier and more efficient.

An observer, fascinated by this concentration of citrus and
bananas, may be led to think that Belize is a veritable paradise rolling
in wealth. To know Belize, however, is to know that is not so. There

is paradisiacal beauty, and there is growing economic development, but Belize is far from being a wealthy nation.

Because SCN experience in Belize began in the Stann Creek District, that district was chosen for the introduction of our story. That district is, however, only one of six into which the country is divided according to its plan of government. (See map on page xviii).

As of the date of this publication, SCNs are serving in Belize City and Stann Creek district. During the past twenty-five years, as succeeding chapters will recount, SCNs have served also in the Cayo and Toledo districts. We have visited the northernmost districts, Corozal and Orange Walk, but have never been in ministry there. Although English is the official language of Belize, Spanish is spoken by many Belizeans, and in some districts Spanish is predominant. Corozal and Orange Walk are two such districts, as might be expected, as they border on Mexico. It is not surprising, then, that a community of women religious from Mexico, the Madrecitas, minister there. We shall meet them in a later chapter.

Chapter Three

SHIFT OF GLOBAL GEARS

At the beginning of the fourth quarter of the twentieth century, the Stann Creek District, just surveyed, was, like the rest of the world, about to experience the groaning of the gears as the earth began to shift into the twenty-first century. It would take every minute of those twenty-five years to make the shift, for nature, even human nature, will not be rushed.

The Catholic Church, in which the Sisters of Charity of Nazareth is a Congregation of women religious founded in Kentucky in 1812, played a prominent part in the transition. The Second Vatican Council—October 11, 1962 to December 8, 1964—was an earthshaking event. Bishop Reuben H. Mueller, President of the National Council of Churches of Christ in the USA, called it "a new adventure in ecumenical cooperation among the followers of our Lord Jesus Christ" (*The Documents of Vatican II*, p. xxi). For those people who looked forward to the immediate implementation of the numerous developments called for by the Council, there have been many disappointments throughout the intervening years. Many wise ones, however, took hold of those prescriptions whose implementation they recognized as not likely to be open to delay and began to move on them immediately. The call for active ministry in the Church by the laity is one of those prescriptions.

The Pastoral Constitution on the Church in the Modern World,
page 244, reads:

> Lay people should also know that it is generally the function of
> their well-informed Christian conscience to see that the divine
> law is inscribed in the life of the earthly city. From priests they
> may look for spiritual light and nourishment. Let the lay men
> and women not imagine that their pastors are always such
> experts that to every problem that arises, however complicated,
> they can readily give a concrete solution or even that such is
> their mission. Rather, enlightened by Christian wisdom and giv-
> ing close attention to the teaching authority of the Church, *let
> the laity take on their own distinctive role* [emphasis added].

It is impossible for SCNs to picture the Church in Belize without lay ministers. It is not true, as many believe, that we were called
to Belize to develop a lay ministry program. We were called there to
assist in a parish, but that call coincided with the worldwide call to
lay ministry and, fortunately, the two calls meshed in Belize.

It was to assist in Sacred Heart Parish in Dangriga that SCNs
were called. The town Dangriga has a long and varied history, as the
previous chapter suggests. At this point in the SCN story, however,
the focus is on the last quarter of the twentieth century—1975-
2000—the period during which the Sisters of Charity of Nazareth
became a part of Belize's history, and the Lay Ministry Program,
deriving from Vatican Council II, became the focus of their ministry.

Before the Council, there had been an emphasis in the Church
on Canon Law. Religious congregations were being called upon to
revise their constitutions, using church law as reference. The Canon
Law Society of America sponsored summer workshops to assist in
that study, and Barbara Thomas, later to become president of the
SCN Congregation, was one of several SCNs who attended the program at Dallas University in Texas. There, in 1966, she met Tom
Swift, SJ, a member of the faculty. Jim Short, SJ, from Belize joined
the faculty the following summer. After the location of the program
was changed to St. Thomas More College in Covington, Kentucky,

both priests continued as members of the staff through 1971. In that year, however, Jim Short was appointed Jesuit Superior in Belize, a position that left him no time for the summer classes. This appointment, coming as it did immediately after his experience in Texas and Kentucky, led him to utilize that experience to help meet one of the early challenges of his administration.

From 1893 until mid twentieth century when several native Belizean men were ordained to the diocesan clergy, all pastors of Roman Catholic churches in Belize were priests of the Society of Jesus (Jesuits) from their St. Louis Province in the United States. By the 1970s, Belize, like every other country, was beginning to experience diminishment in the number of priests available. Those serving the various parishes were becoming concerned about the increasing impossibility of reaching all the people for whom they were responsible as pastors.

The pastor of Sacred Heart Parish in Dangriga, Howard Oliver, SJ, better known as Mike, was one of those concerned pastors. In 1973, he presented his problem to his superior, Jim Short, asking for help in that burgeoning ministry. Jim, knowing that all other priests and religious in the country were occupied full-time in their assigned ministries, began to look for help from beyond immediate boundaries. During a trip to the United States, he phoned Barbara Thomas, then SCN president, with whom he had become acquainted at Dallas University and Thomas More College. Jim presented to her the need in Sacred Heart Parish in Belize, asking her whether there might possibly be SCNs available to minister in Dangriga. Barbara promised to consider his request. At that very time Mary Lynn Fields, SCN, was requesting ministry in India. Barbara had considered her request but found that, at that time, India was not granting long-term visas to Americans. She asked Lynn, therefore, to consider Belize.

Lynn, of course, agreed to go. As noted in a previous chapter, she and Susan Gatz spent the summer of 1974 in Dangriga getting acquainted with the place, and especially with the people, who welcomed them into their homes and into their hearts.

In the meantime, Barbara was concerned about this new venture into which she had led the Community. She realized that accepting a mission in Belize would mean embracing not only a country and a people as yet unfamiliar to SCNs generally, but also a ministry requiring teamwork among women and men of several religious communities with various leadership styles and cultural background differences.

Barbara also understood that the kind of ministry that had been described to her was going to require more than one new SCN working with priests and religious already engaged full time in pastoral work. There would be need for great help from the laity. It was at that point that the Lay Ministry Program began to develop in Dangriga.

Sister of Charity Elizabeth Wendeln and Father Ken Williams (later Bishop Williams of Lexington, Kentucky) were at that time directing the Rural Office of Religious Education in Bardstown, Kentucky. Barbara knew that they had done workshops not only in rural Kentucky but also in Memphis, Tennessee, and at the University of Notre Dame. In them she saw the solution to the need in Belize, and she asked for their assistance. Ken recalls that he and Liz had responded to Barbara's request with some hesitation: "We told her we would consider it." They gave it consideration and much more. With the approval of Archbishop Thomas J. McDonough of the Archdiocese of Louisville, they began designing a model for a workshop to be given in September of 1975 at SCN Center, Nazareth, Kentucky, for a group from Belize.

Reflecting on that experience, Ken says, "I deliberately do not call them a team at this time, since they truly arrived as a group of well-meaning individuals.... We soon realized that persons who were willing to take on such an adventure were obviously independent and strong-minded individuals." Those individuals, according to the files, were Mike Oliver, SJ; Will Charleville, SJ; Mary Lynn Fields, SCN; Barbara Flores (before she entered the SCN Community); another lay person, Dolores Ellis; Marian Joseph Baird, RSM; Rita Mendez, SSF; and Evelyn Estrada, SSF.

One of the best remembered of that group was also the one whose call for help had initiated the entire movement—Mike Oliver. Mike found this new way strange indeed. Yet those who knew him remember him with genuine love and appreciation. Liz speaks of his reverence for people. She calls him "a true missionary, one who planted the seed of lay ministry in Belize." Mike died ten years later, a "true missionary" to the end. He suffered a heart attack while attending a meeting of ministers, lay and religious, at Trinidad Farm in Belize City. He is buried in Belize.

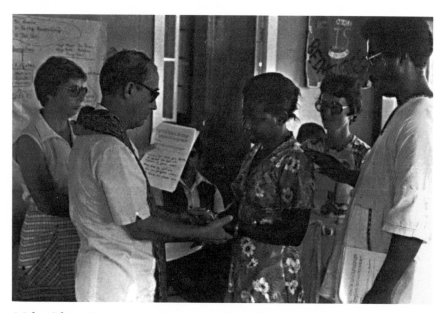

Mike Oliver, SJ, commissions a new lay minister.

Ken recalls the early classes: "We bombarded them with input, reflection, group sharing, role playing. We were always happy to see signs that our efforts were bearing fruit." He tells of one role-playing session when Will Charleville took the role of the parish sister. According to reports, "He painstakingly did his best."

"All of this," Ken says, "was to help the new team members understand where they were with their ecclesiology, the vision of church, the style of leadership out of which they ordinarily operated, organizational skills, communication and conflict resolution skills as well as a basic understanding about how a team ministry could operate. After that first six-week summer session at Nazareth, Kentucky, Liz and Ken received a challenge from the team, "Come to Belize. See us in our own place. Tell us how we're doing here."

Once more, with Archbishop McDonough's blessing, they responded. In 1976 they visited and held workshops in Dangriga. In 1978 they returned to hold a workshop for teams that were developing for the Sacred Heart parishes of San Ignacio in the Cayo District and San Antonio in the Toledo District. Within three years, then, with the encouragement of Bishop Robert L. Hodapp to initiate a lay ministry program in the Diocese of Belize, and with the understanding and encouragement of Archbishop McDonough of Louisville, the team laid the groundwork.

After the summer workshop at Nazareth in 1975, the pastoral team of Dangriga had begun laying plans for the development of lay ministry in the Stann Creek District. They were able to review those plans and have them evaluated in the workshop conducted in Belize in 1977. The *Catholic Bulletin* dated January 9, 1977, listed the pastoral team of Sacred Heart Parish, Dangriga, as follows: Mary Lynn Fields, SCN; Howard C. Oliver, SJ; Kitty Wilson, SCN; Anna Marie Nalley, SCN; Wilfred Charleville, SJ; Evelyn Estrada, SSF; and a layman, Evan Guerrero. The copy of the bulletin on file at Nazareth shows handwritten names of two laywomen—Barbara Flores and Bernadette Arzu.

The bulletin contained three announcements—one about religion classes, one about the reopening of school after the holidays, and one that reads as follows: *The first Ministers of the Word program will be held next weekend Jan.15-16. If anyone interested in participating in the program has not been contacted, please see Sister Lynn very soon.* Those unobtrusive two and one-half lines at the end of a Sunday bulletin assume headline proportions when read in light of the history of the Lay Ministry Program in Belize. The program used several different titles. In Belize City it was "Lay Ministers." Dangriga used the title most like the one in the report from Vatican II, "Ministers of the Word." In some places the ministers were simply called "Catechists."

The program announced for January 15 and 16 was actually a workshop of two days of instruction: a course of studies in all that the ministers would need to know and the methods of teaching that they would have to acquire in order to share the faith with others. A review of the first several sessions reveals some of the content of the course of studies.

From the beginning there was a sound foundation. Charles Hunter, SJ, spoke three times. His topics were "Origins of the People of God," "Introduction to Using the Bible," and "Preparing the Readings of the Day." Music, especially song, was treated by Mike Chesney, SJ, and Evelyn Estrada, SSF. Mike Oliver conducted instruction in public speaking. "We Are People of Prayer" was the session conducted by Kitty Wilson, SCN; Will Charleville, SJ; and Paul White, SJ. SCNs Anna and Kitty held a session on "Communion Services," using the ritual book. Finally, there was a session on "Organization." Lynn conducted the one for villages, Kitty the one for towns. The workshop closed with Liturgy at three o'clock Sunday afternoon.

The following month, February 19-20, 1977, the second session in the series of programs to prepare lay ministers was held. At that session most responsibility rested on members of the pastoral team: Lynn, Kitty, and Mike Oliver. Mike Chesney continued the program in song. This time the group was joined by Sebastian Cayetano, who held a workshop on "Prayer and Song of the Mayas." A core staff continued to conduct the weekend sessions, inviting specialists in fields being stressed at particular seasons. The English language predominated, but Garifuna and Mayan were not neglected.

The program was demanding, meetings being held one weekend each month for ten months. Those sessions required faithful preparation and reports on a certain number of hours of practice each month. The first group of ministers for the Stann Creek District completed preparation by the end of 1977. After a three-day retreat at Pelican Beach, they were commissioned by Bishop Hodapp in Sacred Heart Church on New Year's Day, 1978.

Meanwhile similar programs were developing throughout the country. Directors of those programs in several districts were profiting from the workshops conducted by Liz and Ken. The original call of SCNs to Belize was the call to pastoral ministry. It became almost immediately a call to assist in developing the ministry of the laity. No program stands alone, however. In the spring of 1978, Anita Hager, SCN, spent six weeks in Dangriga setting up the library at Ecumenical High School. She unboxed the books and shelved them. In order to complete the task, however, she needed materials and facilities that were not immediately available. She returned home, therefore, and with the assistance of Spalding University and Presentation Academy and the help of Jean Gish she completed the task.

Related to lay ministry were other types of education as well as various kinds of health care. Frequently, however, those who served in other programs served also in the preparation of lay ministers. For example, listed among those in that first parish team in Dangriga in 1977 is Anna Marie Nalley, SCN, a nurse-practitioner employed full time by the Health Department of Belize. Anna was also a member of the staff of that first two-day ministers' workshop.

Anna's participation in the Lay Ministry Program did not interfere with her ministry in the profession of nursing. In fact the two were often related, as the following story illustrates. Anna says: "I first met Ronald in the pediatric ward of the Dangriga Hospital where he had been abandoned—dying from malnutrition. He lay in a bed without care, waiting for death. 'At least he should die with a full stomach,' I thought."

Anna then tells how, after she gave him a bottle of milk and he continued to live, the staff began to take an interest in him. The baby, who was between twelve and eighteen months old, weighed only twelve pounds. Anna continued to feed him during the day, and the night nurses cared for him at night.

"It was three weeks before he cried," says Anna, "and a month before he could roll over in bed, but Ronald lived. In October, two months after being left there, he pulled himself up in his crib, and the nurses sent for me to 'Come quick!' Fearing the worst, I ran over from the Health Center, only to find the staff each wanting to be the first to tell me about Ronald's standing up."

Anna says that after that she frequently took him home with her, and in November he shared their baked chicken for Thanksgiving. Then one day she received word to come and pick up Ronald who was "well enough to go home."

"It was only then that I learned that the magistrate had legally 'given' me Ronald. No protests made any difference, so Ronald came home with me," she continues.

Anna fixed a pallet for the baby on the floor in her room. She recalls observing how quickly he learned. She recalls too her concern about finding a family for him, for she knew that she could not keep him.

Recalling that Sebastian and Isabelle Cayetano in Belize City were heartbroken over having just lost their second child at birth, Anna called them and asked if they wanted to adopt Ronald. She told them that the child's background was a mixture of Garifuna and East Indian. Overnight they decided to make Ronald their own.

A week before Christmas 1979, Lynn took Ronald to Belize City. Lynn, who had business there, would ordinarily have driven, but the roads were flooded, so Ronald had an early experience of a flight to Belize City, a flight to meet his parents.

Anna says, "There were many tears shed by us and by the priests, Mike Oliver and John Waters, for the child had grown deep into our hearts. The pastoral team had Christmas dinner that day and Ronald was dressed in a red and white outfit, looking like a little Santa."

When Lynn and Anna were preparing dinner, they missed Mike and Ronald. Anna found them on the front veranda. Mike was holding Ronald and talking to him. He was telling Ronald to look out at the world as it was there before him to take hold of, and to be something.

He told him that he was given a special chance at life and he just needed to reach out and take it. Anna quietly withdrew into the house, and Mike never knew that she had heard a word.

Anna recalls that when Ronald was leaving, John Waters walked away with tears in his eyes, "and that's not surprising," she says. "When he would baby-sit, John often rode Ronald on his shoulders through Dangriga as he made his parish visits."

At the other end of the journey in Belize City, Izzy and Sebastian were waiting at the airport, unsure whether or not their decision was wise. Lynn said that when she got off the plane with Ronald "he held out his hands to Izzy, and all doubt vanished."

They took Ronald home and loved him. They changed his name to Carlos, and in a few years he had two little brothers. Whether or not he had understood what Mike had said to him, the turn of the century found him, a high school graduate, studying to become a chef, a field in which he is decidedly talented.

Meanwhile, that first ceremony in Dangriga to commission lay ministers marked an important step in the development of SCN ministry in Belize. Even while the first Stann Creek candidates were being commissioned, groups in other districts were preparing for similar ceremonies.

When Vatican II, as we usually call the Second Vatican Council, was drawing to a close in December 1964, confirmed optimists like me began looking immediately for fulfillment of all that it had promised. Wiser folk, however, reminded me, "It will take at least a century. History unfolds gradually." As I mark off the years, if I am tempted to become discouraged, I say to myself, "Look at the ministry of the laity. It is far from reaching its peak in numbers or activities, but in some places it has continued to grow and to be very faithful and very active." I also remind myself that it took a decade for it to get under way. Vatican II closed in 1964; our story opened with a prelude in the summer of 1974. That story continues with an account of a violent storm and of serious civil disturbance in the fall of 1978.

Chapter Four

STORMS:
TROPICAL AND POLITICAL

The newly commissioned ministers had just begun to practice
their work, and classes for the next group had begun, when
the serenity of life in Dangriga was interrupted in the fall of
that same year, 1978, by a serious hurricane. No loss of life occurred,
but the country suffered extreme damage, especially to the banana
and citrus crops, so important to the economy of Belize. The house
where the SCNs lived was among those most likely to withstand the
wind, so they invited a number of people to join them. The storm
broke about 7:30 p.m. on September 18.

Anna Marie Nalley, SCN, was stationed at the emergency hospital, located at the office of the town board. There, at the peak of
the storm, the doors were torn off and the furniture hurled around
the room. Anna returned home about four o'clock in the morning,
but soon went out again—this time in a helicopter—to check the villages. She found no injuries, but she had to return later to give
immunization injections against typhoid. She reported that there was
no running water in the villages and that many homes had been damaged and some destroyed. Those whose homes had withstood the
storm were housing their less fortunate neighbors as well as their
own families. The crowded conditions were not good, but no one
complained, so grateful were they that they had survived.

Even in the larger villages it would be several weeks before life would return to normal. Mary Lynn Fields, SCN, wrote to Nazareth: "For a while our only outside contact was the helicopter that dropped emergency supplies." Belize had suffered more devastating hurricanes in 1931 and 1961. Belizeans were relieved, therefore, that Hurricane Greta, despite its seriousness, had caused no fatalities.

Still more frightening than the hurricane was the human reaction in April 1981 to reports that independence of Belize from Britain was about to become a reality. Despite the tendency on the part of Britain at that time to encourage colonies desiring independence to move in that direction, Belize, out of fear, had by choice remained a colony.

It was not any lack of self-esteem or of confidence in ability to govern that had held the country back. In fact, there had been within the country for many years a movement toward independence strong enough to develop a functioning internal government based on a two-party system. Hesitancy on the part of Belize to move toward independence stemmed from an old Guatemalan claim that the 8,886 square-mile area known as Belize was actually part of Guatemala. As long as Belize should remain a colony of England, that country would prevent a Guatemalan takeover. The new country of Belize had a defense force, but it was neither large enough nor strong enough to compete with Guatemalan forces.

The dispute is an old one. It does not prevent Belizeans from going across the border into neighboring Guatemala. All that is required is to stop at the government building on the border to have one's passport stamped, as is required upon entry into any foreign country.

One aspect of the process in Guatemala, however, is particularly alarming to Belizeans. People waiting in line with their passports face a mural depicting the map of Guatemala that includes all of Belize—the Caribbean, the rain forest, the barrier reef, the Maya Mountains, all the towns and villages, with no mention of the name Belize.

It is not surprising, then, that there was widespread concern when, on March 16, 1981, there was an announcement in Guatemala, Britain, and Belize that the resolution of the previous year in the United Nations regarding Belize's independence would be carried out. Accompanying the announcement was the publication of what were called "Heads of Agreement" that were interpreted by some in Belize as the conditions for independence, whereas they really described a process for the changeover.

In writing to Dorothy MacDougall, President of the Sisters of Charity of Nazareth, Lynn stated, "I think there was a basic misunderstanding of the meaning of 'Heads of Agreement.'" Evidently the term was indicative of a list of agenda for developing a treaty, but the opposition refused to be quelled. There was great unrest and destruction of property. Belize, which had always been a peaceful country, had become disrupted and painfully dangerous. Bishop Hodapp, ordinarily a very quiet man, spoke out against the violence, and the violence was turned against the Church.

A fire set in Lynn's office on the ground floor of the rectory was discovered before the wooden structure could catch fire, but the threat was alarming. No one knew whom to trust. The upheaval continued, but gradually became less violent. By the time the actual conditions of independence were completed, explained, and accepted by all parties, it was agreed that the fears of the opposition were not justified. In addition, Britain gave assurance of leaving a contingent of the air force in the country until such time as the problem with Guatemala might be resolved. Twenty years later, the problem continues, but current reports suggest the possibility of a solution in sight.

To know Belize it is necessary to know what the Guatemala problem is and to understand why some Belizeans would let it stand in the way of independence. After the mysterious disappearance of the Maya from the country that had been their homeland for centuries, Belize became a haven for bandits and rovers of all kinds, even though there is evidence that some people may have made a home there. By the fifteenth century Europe became interested in the area, as North Americans know. We have all heard about how Columbus, landing in Central America and thinking that he was in India, called the islands of the Caribbean the West Indies and the people in the area Indians, a mistake that has been perpetuated "officially." Some people from India, however, notably some SCNs, say that they can recognize similarities between the Maya and themselves. There is a theory that at some unrecorded period of history people from India crossed the Bering Strait and came down through the area that is now Canada, the United States, and Mexico and settled in what is currently Central America.

Whatever may be the ancient history, the 1500s saw the Spanish in Guatemala and the British on the high seas becoming interested in the beauty and the fruitfulness of the land that is now Belize. Spain was the first to set out to take the land from the native people. Assad Shoman, in *Thirteen Chapters of a History of Belize,* p. 10, describes the cruelty of the Spanish when the native people resisted enslavement. The British supplemented that population with shiploads of Africans whom they forced from their native land, bringing them over to work in the newly discovered fields and forests.

Competition for the land continued until 1798, when, on September 10 of that year, a single British schooner, assisted by "a ragged band of Baymen" (Belizeans), overcame "seasoned Spanish naval forces." The Battle of St. George's Caye is described by Belizeans from various points of view. Zee Edgell, a very successful Belizean writer, has Granny Ivy in the novel *Beka Lamb* say, "Belize people liked to remember the battle because it was one of the few things attempted in the country that hadn't broken down" (p. 46). Regardless of one's attitude, however, September 10 is a national holiday in Belize, matching in spirit any celebration of July 4 that citizens of the United States have ever seen. The outcome of the Battle of St. George's Caye also explains why English is the national language of Belize, whereas Spanish is the national language of all the other Central-American countries.

In 1823 James Monroe, President of the United States, stated that the USA opposed further European colonization of or intervention in the Western Hemisphere. Known as the Monroe Doctrine, the document was neither contested nor fully accepted. For example, in 1850 Britain agreed to refrain from fortifying, occupying, or colonizing any part of Central America, but maintained that, because of a former settlement, the treaty exempts British Honduras, as Belize was then called. Nine years later Guatemala recognized British sovereignty but claimed and continues to claim that it did so because Britain had agreed to build a road through the contested land to the Caribbean coast. That road was never built, and periodically Guatemala uses the situation as a threat to Belize. In 1981, however, despite delays that resulted from fear of Guatemala, Belize moved on to independence.

In recognition of this important event in the history of Belize and in order to ask a special blessing on the country and its people, Bishop Hodapp, on Sunday, September 20, 1981, with Papal Nuncio Archbishop Paul Tabet and Monsignor Preston Moss, Vicar General of Nassau in the Bahamas, concelebrated Mass in Holy Redeemer Cathedral. According to the *Christian Herald,* the cathedral was filled to capacity as were the extensive grounds surrounding it.

The headline story in the *Belize Sunday Times*, September 27, 1981, reads as follows:

> Independence came to Belize at midnight Sept. 20 as the British flag, the Union Jack, was lowered at Government House Yard while the Belizean flag was hoisted, and at the stroke of twelve the spotlight came on. A member of the Belize Defense Force pulled a cord, causing the flag to unfurl majestically amid applause by some 1000 people gathered around the base of the mast.

His Royal Highness Prince Michael delivered the Proclamation of Independence, and Prime Minister George Price responded: "This symbolic transition to the independent state of Belize signifies the

Holy Redeemer Cathedral

fulfillment of decolonization which, as a metropolitan country and founding member of the United Nations, the United Kingdom undertook to accomplish under the charter."

The *Times* pointed out that Belize, "now the 156th member of the United Nations," was the last British colony on the Central-American mainland, and that the transition "deserves the admiration of all peaceful, freedom-loving nations." The *Times* continues:

> In the morning at Belmopan, the lately established capital, His Royal Highness Prince Michael of Kent, representing his first cousin, Queen Elizabeth Second of England, formally handed over the constitutional instruments for the independent nation of Belize and announced amid cheers that Belize had that day become the forty-fifth member of the Commonwealth.

Present at the ceremony were Dr. Minita Gordon, Governor General of Belize, and Mr. Nicholas Ridley, representative of the British Government.

A message to Prime Minister Price from Pope John Paul II read as follows: "As you celebrate national independence, I offer my best wishes to Your Excellency and all the people of Belize." The Prime Minister responded:

> On behalf of the people of Belize, please accept our deep gratitude for your message. . . . Please accept our assurance that the independent Belize will continue to work for peace, stability, and prosperity in the Caribbean and Central-American region as we live our constitution which enshrines the principles of justice, freedom, and integral human development.

A week later, at the meeting of the United Nations, according to the *Times*, "Jean Kirkpatrick, the United States Ambassador to the UN, was the first to congratulate Prime Minister Price after Belize was admitted as the 156th member of the world body." Then followed the ambassadors from the United Kingdom, Mexico, Nicaragua, Ghana, and a line of delegates who took twenty minutes to congratulate and welcome Belize in the person of Prime Minister George Price.

Every year Belize celebrates Independence Day, September 21, with parades, fireworks, picnics of all kinds, and with prayers of thanksgiving. To leave the story there, however, without mentioning once more the Guatemala question, would be failing to be realistic.

The *Times,* in reporting the vote of the Security Council, September 23, stated that the Council "voted to approve Belize as the 156th member of the United Nations. Guatemala opposed, but was overruled." In the United States the Associated Press released a statement: "Guatemala tells UN it will not recognize independent Belize." A headline in *Time* magazine, Oct. 5, 1981, reads "Free but Vulnerable." And so it has remained for more than twenty years.

During those years opinions and attitudes have differed. Some people have said that the issue is dead and that Guatemala has no further interest in a road through Belize to the sea. Others have maintained that such issues never die. When some incident recalls it to memory, such as a recent holdup of a bus in Belize by bandits whose car bore a Guatemalan license, the ghost rears its head again. At such times Britain lets it be known that it is not far away.

A colony of Britain since 1862 and known as British Honduras, Belize, in spite of the Guatemalan problem, had long been preparing for independence. In 1973, while still a colony, it became known as Belize and recognized as a constitutional monarchy, functioning as a parliamentary democracy. The Prime Minister, with the aid of ten cabinet ministers, carries out the operation of the government. The National Assembly, consisting of the twenty-eight-member House of Representatives and the eight-member Senate, makes the country's laws.

The people elect the House members. The leader of the party that wins the most seats in the House serves as Prime Minister. The Governor General, a Belizean, representing the British Monarch, approves the eight senators on advice of the majority party in the house. Two senators are appointed on advice of the minority party; another senator is appointed on recommendation of the Governor General's advisory council.

The two parties, the People's United Party (PUP) and the United Democratic Party (UDP), are active political organizations. Elections, scheduled by the party in office, take place ordinarily every four years. Before independence the PUP, led by George Price, was the party in power. With independence, parties have alternated frequently.

At the turn of the millennium, January 2000, the old problem with Guatemala surfaced once more. At that time all parties agreed that "This time it must be resolved." Eighteen months later, July 22, 2001, the *Reporter*, one of Belize's many newspapers, carried a story reported below in summary.

The two countries have agreed to put the question into the hands of facilitators, Sir Shridath Ramphal for Belize and attorney Paul Reichler for Guatemala. The two facilitators have agreed to present proposals by December 15, 2001. Both sides have accepted the facilitators' recommendations that they pursue a definitive solution via the facilitation process and that the time frame for the process be extended a year to August 31, 2002. Those recommendations were presented to their respective delegations meeting July 18 at the headquarters of the Organization of American States in Washington, D.C.

Senior Ambassador Assad Shoman, returning to Belize July 19, said, "Unlike previous occasions, what may result from this process is not through a negotiation between two sides, where we sit at the same table and talk about recommendations and suggestions. The facilitators will be in constant communication and consultation with the two parties."

Ambassador Shoman explained that when the facilitators' proposal is ready it will be brought home to the people and there will be consultation on it. He admitted, however, that the facilitators have no easy job. He added that both the United States and the United Kingdom "have been very supportive of this process." Regrettably, the possible date of the outcome of that process is later than the date proposed for the publication of this book. Since the latter date is approaching rapidly, it is necessary to move from the Caribbean coast westward toward hills and towering Maya ruins.

Chapter Five

LAY MINISTRY: A DECADE OF ACHIEVEMENT

S CN presence in San Ignacio is one of the results of *Justice 75*, a program inaugurated in the United States to give SCNs and others an opportunity to volunteer for ministry in areas anywhere in the world not then served by the Community. Belize is only an hour or two away from places in the United States where many SCNs were living when the program began, much closer than many had realized. For a number of years the usual trip has been a two-hour flight from Miami, New Orleans, or Houston over the Gulf of Mexico to Belize City. Those who have gone by land in car or truck have traveled from four to seven days, depending on whether they have done any traveling at night. Many are surprised to find that it would be possible to cross the border immediately from Mexico into Belize—from North America to Central America—without being aware of doing so, were it not for diligent customs officers stationed there.

After spending the summer of 1976 in San Ignacio with a Franciscan sister, Luanne Schenzele, Judy Raley, SCN, returned two years later with another SCN, Kitty Wilson. They were ready to become part of an ongoing mission, a pastoral team, in San Ignacio's Sacred Heart Parish. There they joined two priests, Jack Ruoff, SJ, and Herb Panton, and two women religious, SACs Stephen Franco and Josella Flowers.

*Kitty Wilson
conveys a message
to other pastoral
team members
in San Ignacio—
Herb Panton,
Jack Ruoff, SJ,
and Stephen
Franco, SAC.*

An article by Judy Raley in the *Christian Herald*, November 18, 1979, gives an account of the team's first year. A meeting had been held September 7 of that year to evaluate the accomplishment of the goals set forth the year before. The report of that meeting, on file in the archives at Nazareth, states in detail what had been done toward accomplishing each of the goals: spiritual, educational, social, cultural, and administrative. Anyone reading that report is bound to wish that the meeting had been videotaped rather than typed, realizing, nevertheless, that video cameras were not as numerous nor as easy to operate in 1978 as they are today.

That the structure of the plan for the pastoral team at Sacred Heart Church, San Ignacio, in 1978-1979 was both logical and comprehensive is evident to anyone who has the patience to read it. It requires patience because it is detailed, as any plan involving so many people individually and in groups has to be. Judy, the author of the plan, wasted no words, and she presented it in outline form that is easy to follow. No person or thing is omitted: everyone close at hand and everyone in the most distant village of the parish; every religious service in the church and every organization of the parish;

every social aspect of the lives of the people, with special emphasis on education. Even relationship with external groups is handled. There are even references to delegates to the Diocesan Assembly and to a booth at the National Agricultural Fair. This brief summary hardly does justice to the plan that closes with a statement of the cultural goal:

> our mission is to a Belizean Church and therefore to strive systematically in all our activities to question ourselves and others on whether what is being done is a proper Gospel response to Belizean needs, and a good Belizean response to the Gospel.

The team spent little time looking at past accomplishments, however. Plans that were made for the year 1979-1980 included preparing detailed job descriptions for every member. In the meantime, Judy had agreed to be responsible for developing the Lay Ministry Program for Sacred Heart Parish that served two towns and seven villages. Early in 1980 thirty-seven men and women began the yearlong preparation for becoming lay ministers.

At the same time the government of Belize was negotiating with the government of Great Britain to become separate from that country, of which it had been a colony for more than a century. As mentioned in the preceding chapter, not all Belizeans were happy about the impending change. Reaction in Cayo was not as violent as in Dangriga, however, and when Britain agreed to leave protective troops in the country for a while, the district went about its business confidently. The development of lay ministers was part of that business. Each year for the next several years the ministers who had spent the year in preparation were commissioned. Those already commissioned and working successfully in ministry were reconfirmed. Lay ministers were growing in self-confidence and were conducting prayer and communion services in the villages. They visited the sick and brought them Holy Communion, assisted in preparation for First Communion and Confirmation, planned liturgies and prayer services, and conducted funerals in the absence of a priest.

Meanwhile Kitty was working in two other important ministries. She was helping teachers to improve the teaching of religion in the school, and directing "Search," a program for the young people of the parish. One of those young people was Amina Bejos, who worked in both "Search" and lay ministry. Amina came naturally by her apostolic spirit. Her grandmother is Dona Elena, a well-known fiery lay leader of San Ignacio. Amina soon entered the Nazareth Novitiate and was professed as a Sister of Charity in 1987. As the community prepared to celebrate twenty-five years in Belize during the Jubilee Year 2000, Amina was directing a "Search" program in Kentucky, where she is a member of the faculty of Lexington Catholic High School.

The "Search" program is a retreat in which young people themselves, guided by well-prepared adults, lead the movement of the group. Lynn introduced the program in Dangriga. She had been one of the adult guides in such a program at Memphis Catholic High School. When in 1978 she arranged for a student-exchange program between that school and the high school in Dangriga, "Search" was part of the program. Kitty introduced it in Sacred Heart High School in San Ignacio. It is interesting to see how a valuable tool, well handled, can enrich generations from state to state and country to country. Recently, at the invitation of Irene Locario, SCN, Amina brought students from Lexington, Kentucky, to St. Catherine Academy in Belize City to assist with the "Search" program there.

Amina has taken other groups from the States to Belize, through a program that gives the young people in the schools in the two countries an opportunity to become acquainted with one another and with the school system in the "other" country. For example, visiting students are given an opportunity to teach mathematics or reading, or whatever may be the subject preferred. The Belizeans observe the visitors' presentations, and the visitors the response of the Belizeans.

It is not only schools that Amina's groups visit, however. For example, they assist in HelpAge, a program for the elderly, established in several areas of the country. They go to Mercy Clinic and

Mercy Kitchen, conducted by the Sisters of Mercy for the assistance of the poor. It is not only groups of her own students that Amina takes to Belize. She and SCN Luke Boiarski took a group of students to Belize from Tiltonsville, Ohio, the scene of Luke's ministry. Besides sharing in several classes, they also shared a program called "Youth Enrichment." Genuine education, at whatever age, is truly an experience of enrichment.

The Lay Ministry Program in which Judy and Kitty were involved is an equally enriching experience. Judy and the ministers had been busy, not only with their usual responsibilities but also with plans for the first national gathering of lay ministers. The Lay Ministry Program had developed well since its beginning nearly a decade earlier. It was evident, however, that there was a growing need for the many local groups of ministers to come together, to recognize one another and to be recognized by others as a national organization in the Church of Belize. That recognition would strengthen the foundation of their ministry and make known their availability to serve as well as the manner in which they are prepared to serve.

Nancy Kaelin, SCN, Moderator for the Youth Group of Sacred Heart Parish in San Ignacio, reviews with Isaura Chuc and SCN Irene Locario plans for coming events.

A growing awareness of the need to bring all the teams together had been developing among the leaders. When, therefore, the leaders in San Ignacio offered to host a national meeting, the response was genuinely enthusiastic. Bishop Osmond P. Martin agreed to open the meeting and to remain for the two days. Priests, men and women religious, members of the laity marked their calendars and began looking forward to the event.

That first national gathering of lay ministers, scheduled to be held March 9-11, 1984, in San Ignacio at the San Ignacio Hotel, was sponsored by the Diocese and planned by all the lay ministers and their directors. The implementation of the plans naturally fell chiefly to those in San Ignacio. The planners wisely began their work months in advance. As the time for the gathering approached, they went to the management of the hotel to confirm their reservations. In doing so they found that indeed the San Ignacio Hotel had listed the Lay Ministry Program, reserving for that program a certain number of rooms and a large meeting room. The management congratulated the planners on having made their reservations well in advance, for since they had done so a larger group had applied for similar space. Fortunately, the hotel was large enough to accommodate both groups. When they inquired about the identity of the larger group, however, the ministry planners recognized it as a very respectable organization but one that by its very nature was very noisy, and they knew that neither the assembly room nor the sleeping rooms were soundproof. They realized that their foresight had been rewarded with accommodations, but accommodations that they could not use. Because there was no other large hotel in the area, the planners were faced with some fast readjustment of plans.

The outcome of a prayerful meeting of the committee was a decision to request help from the British army, still encamped protectively near the airport in Belize City. Judy went to the proper officials, presented the problem, and asked for help. In response the army offered a gigantic tent together with soldiers to erect it and to check it every day in order to insure the safety of the people who would be seated within it. The soldiers assigned to that duty were Gurkhas, a special group of men in the British army. Those soldiers have a history with particular appeal to SCNs because of the SCN connection with Nepal, the Gurkhas' country of origin.

The tent furnished by the British army and erected and maintained by Gurkhas—soldiers in the army of Nepal— saved the day when hotel reservations proved unsatisfactory.

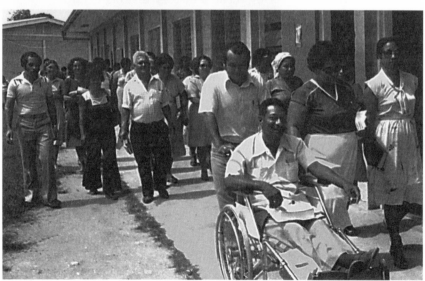

One group of Lay Ministers moves toward the tent.

Gurkhas are short, muscular, very strong men. At one time in the history of Nepal, when Britain was in control in India, there was trouble between Nepal and their neighbors in India. Part of a peace settlement was an agreement that Nepal would supply a certain number of men for the British army. It was further agreed that that number be chosen from the world-renowned Gurkhas, natives of one of the independent principalities ruling Nepal in 1860.

SCN Ann Kernen remembers a conversation that she had with two Gurkhas at a bus stop several years later. Recalling words that she had learned while she had been missioned in Nepal, she greeted the two young men in her best Nepalese. They looked puzzled and asked her to repeat, and she did so. Then one responded, "Sorry, Sister, we don't speak Spanish."

The *SCNews*, March 1984, carried an account of the National Gathering, reporting that 255 lay ministers and catechists from all six districts of Belize attended March 9-11. Six months later *SCN Mission News* likewise reported on the Gathering. Using the two reports to stimulate as well as to verify our memories, those of us who attended the Gathering recall a history-making event.

Belize's Bishop Martin opened the Gathering Friday evening, as pointed out earlier, calling the attention of his audience to their stated purpose: "to reflect, to share experiences, and to write a position paper, presenting to the Church of Belize their vision of the role of the laity."

SCNews stated that thirty-nine Mayan lay ministers and catechists from San Luis Rey Parish in the Toledo District attended together with a group from Punta Gorda, accompanied by John Loretto, SCN. Three other SCNs—Sarah Ferriell, Lynn Fields, and Judy Raley—together with representatives from lay ministry programs in Dangriga, Belize City, Cayo, Corozal, and Punta Gorda, had been planning the event since October. Like the annual Chicago meeting on which it was patterned, it was simply called "The Gathering." Leaders were prepared to guide discussion and the preparation of the position paper.

A newspaper account reminded me that I had prepared a presentation entitled "The Church in Belize," using slides of lay ministers and their activities in the various districts. Enthusiastic narration, by Charles Hunter, SJ, on "The Young Church of Belize," accompanied the slides.

Hunter, a Belizean himself, said, "With independence from Britain in 1981 and the ordination of the diocese's first Belizean-born bishop the following year, it is appropriate to speak of 'the young Church of Belize,' as leadership of the Church passes into the hands of Belizeans" (pp.10-12).

Keynote speaker for the occasion was internationally known Anthony Bellagamba, IMC, of the United States Mission Conference, better known as Father Tony. That he did much more than sound the keynote is revealed by the list of topics he addressed at various intervals throughout the three days: "The Call and Challenge of Lay Ministry" and "The Call of the Church in a Global Society." Quotations from those talks in *SCN Mission News* are just as valid and challenging today as they were fifteen years ago; for example, "Up to 1970 the majority of Catholics were in Europe and North America; now they are in Africa, Asia, Latin and Central America and Oceania. Currently, 60% of the world's Catholics are in those countries."

Speaking to the lay ministers, he said, "Here is where your ministry is important. Here is where you can do a lot to build God's Kingdom here on earth, which is run, not by power but by service, whose members are committed to each other and to the rest of the world." The term kingdom will offend many readers today because of its political connotation. Only a few would have objected to its use twenty years ago. The very fact that Tony stressed service in contrast to power is evidence that habit, not preference, motivated his choice of words.

He stressed especially that "The main preoccupation of the Global Church is the building of the kingdom . . . life in all of its manifestations, the total welfare of human beings. It is mission. The

Father Tony Bellagamba, IMC (in the checked shirt), kneeling in the front row, is surrounded by lay ministers. He did much more than sound the keynote of the conference. He called the newly commissioned ministers to service. "The main purpose of the Global Church," he said, "is the total welfare of human beings."

Whether speaking to the assembled ministers, enjoying breaks with them, or offering Mass with them, Tony Bellagamba personified the organization that he represented—the United States Mission Conference. It was evident that he had at heart "the total welfare of human beings," and he inspired his audience to make that their concern too.

Church does not exist for itself; it exists for others, for the kingdom." Here it is even more evident that the word *kingdom* is meant to imply "the total welfare of human beings" (pp. 4, 6).

The program for the Gathering carries fourteen lists of fifteen to twenty people each, with leaders indicated, for discussion of the topics presented, all of them treating some aspect of Lay Ministry. There are also other groups listed to make special presentations; for example, Sarita Vasquez, RSM, Mr. Evaraldo Puc, and Charles Hunter, SJ, formed a panel to lead off discussion toward the development of a position paper.

The well organized meeting not only carried out its carefully made plans but also met successfully the emergencies presented by lack of hotel space for sleeping and for food service. Groups of good cooks, under the leadership of Josella Flowers, SAC, came together to make some festive meals for the entire group. For weeks prior to The Gathering, lay ministers from Cayo visited members of the parish asking whether they might offer hospitality to the visitors. The response was overwhelming; some 200 people were accommodated.

Whether in her role as volunteer food manager for an assembly of 200 people, as an enthusiastic participant in that assembly, or as "apostle of the road (see page 153)," SAC Josella Flowers fills the role to perfection.

As was clear from the beginning, one of the chief goals of pastoral teamwork was the development of lay ministry. The next chapter will reveal how well that goal was reached and maintained in spite of difficulties encountered in keeping that ministry alive. Of the original team, only Josella was still in San Ignacio in 1997. Many of the people whom they prepared for lay ministry, however, are continuing to minister, and others have joined them. Leadership is in the hands of Belizeans.

When, in 1981, Belize became independent, celebrations continued throughout the year. One of the events in the schools was the circulation of the famous Jade Head. Here SCN Judy Raley, under the watchful eye of the exhibit official, holds the famous relic briefly on exhibit at Sacred Heart College, San Ignacio (see also Chapter 10, p. 114).

Chapter Six

EVANGELIZERS

Since her days as a member of the San Ignacio team, Judy Raley has answered the call to leadership, first as Vice-president of the SCN Congregation, then as Vice-president for Mission at Memorial Healthcare System in Chattanooga, Tennessee. As homilist at Nazareth, Kentucky, on Mission Sunday 1996, she recalled her days in San Ignacio.

Quoting from the mission statement of the Congregation, reminding us that "to evangelize we must be evangelized," she said, "I'd like to introduce to you some people who have been my evangelizers." From the many whom Judy had known, she chose three whose circumstances and special gifts illustrated her purpose well:

> I can still hear Neya singing as she bent over her washboard each day. As her song echoed across the hills of San Ignacio she witnessed to God's presence in her life. I saw her tremendous faith when her twenty-year-old daughter became disabled as the result of a brain tumor. Neya was attuned to the voices of those in need as she walked the hills of San Ignacio each week to bring Eucharist and to share the power of God acting in her life.

Next Judy spoke of Teody, a constant reminder that it is " God who is in control." She told of one occasion when

> several of our parish ministers were going to a liturgical conference in Trinidad. On the way to the airport it was discovered

that one of them didn't have required travel documents. The pastor was irritated and wanted to send the person back home. Amid the consternation and bewilderment of the group, Teody called them to stop and pray and then consider what they might do. I don't know what the solution was; they found one and everyone went to Trinidad.

Judy's third "evangelizer" was Maria, single parent of a disabled child:

> She had little by way of material resources, but she was rich in spiritual ones. She is one of those people whose radiant countenance and caring demeanor make you feel special. She cared for the church in its people and its building. She gathered a group of women to keep the church clean and had the altar ready for liturgy each week. She saw the face of God in all she met, and I saw the face of God in Maria.

Judy introduced those women of Cayo so convincingly that any one hearing her must have felt certain that she would recognize them all if it were possible to meet them. I did recognize them when, a few months later, I visited Belize once more. In Cayo I found Neya, Teody, Maria, and some of their friends who, like them, are filled with enthusiasm for sharing the word of God. Judy had described them very well.

In her homily, Judy had mentioned Neya's daughter who had survived the removal of a tumor from her brain. I had met the young woman, Ycela, shortly after her surgery and had marveled at the spirit that was sustaining her in spite of some post-operative side effects. When I visited her this time, after more than a decade, I found her in a wheelchair, the result of a fall that had left her with a broken hip that is not likely to heal completely.

Ycela teaches religion at Sacred Heart School. Her specialty is preparation of students for the reception of the sacraments. She used to hold her classes in the school that is very near her home. Now, however, because she lacks easy mobility, the students come to the living room of her home.

Ycela maintains her enthusiasm for life, for her faith, for people. As we talked, she began asking about people who have been in ministry in San Ignacio. She did not hesitate for a name. She remembers each one as an individual and loves every one of them; and she says, "I love my Church and I love my country."

Ycela was the first among several teachers whom I interviewed in San Ignacio. I was staying with the Pallottine Sisters, and Sister Josella, who had at heart my interest in writing this book, lost no opportunity to have me meet a number of people who generously shared information that opened for me a window on many aspects of Belize.

Thanks to Josella, I had a visit to the Mayan Tanah Art Museum. The museum is part of a compound on which live the Garcia sisters, their brothers, their parents, and an extended family. There, in 1983, still in their teens, as they were working one day in the field, one of them picked up a piece of slate. They say that they were "inspired" to carve the rock into a whale. "This inspiration came from the heart and soul as the artists awakened to the tradition of slate carving, lost since the ancient days of Corozal around 613 A.D." A brochure describing the Garcia sisters' work is filled with convincing information: "Driven

One of the Garcia sisters works on her carving.

to understand the ways of their ancestors, the sisters seek out the elders of their community as well as archeological experts in order to create authentic Mayan art." The Garcia sisters' address is P. O. Box 75, San Ignacio, Cayo District, Belize.

One of the generous people mentioned by Josella was Bernadine Avila, a teacher for more than thirty years. For many of those years she taught in the Infant School (in the English system, the first and second grades). Now she teaches special education in standard three (grade five). There are thirty-seven students in regular classrooms. Ms. Avila has twenty-seven.

Talking with Bernadine in the quiet parlor of the Pallottine convent one afternoon, I asked her, "As Belize develops, are there changes in the school system?"

Bernadine responded with a definite "Yes." She continued, "When I started teaching I was fresh from primary school. If you were diligent enough, you qualified yourself. Now even a college graduate is not qualified until after probation."

Some thirty years ago, Bernadine started at $27.00 (US) a week, she told me. Now, with a diploma, the beginning salary is $75.00 (US) a week. The maximum salary is $900.00 (US) a month. Retirement benefits are given in a lump sum by agreement according to the salary at retirement time. (Two Belizean dollars equal one American dollar.) This veteran teacher says that the arrangement is not bad but not all that it should be. For example, the more benefits, the more demands; and there is nothing extra for managing extracurricular activities.

Bernadine reminded me that there is no public school system as such. Most of the schools are church-related. The Belize government pays fifty percent of the overhead cost of operating them. The government pays the salaries of the teachers in all elementary schools and seventy-five percent of the salaries of the teachers in all high schools. The government also pays the tuition of students at all levels.

As I showed Bernadine to the door and watched her go down the steep hill toward the town, I reflected on the women with whom I had been talking the last few days: Teody, Neya, Maria, Ycela,

Bernadine, and others in that San Ignacio band of lay ministers. They are all so different from one another in personality, circumstances, age, and education. What they have in common is a strong faith and a desire to share it. When Bishop Robert L. Hodapp gave his blessing to the ministry team in 1979, he facilitated their efforts by making public the need of and respect for lay leadership in his diocese.

The first recruits, many of whom are the present veterans, were ready for the call, for many of them had been in prayer groups and had been ministering to the sick and the dying. Their pastors, like the Bishop, could see that the Church and the people needed them. Time has proved that pastors and bishop were right.

The Church continues to call on those people. Francisca Jones, with whom I talked, said, "Father Richard asked me to invite people to Mass in the monastery. I did, and sometime there isn't room for them all, especially during Lent." Francisca made a simple comparison. She said, "It's like the priests cook dinner and we invite the people in to enjoy it."

Francisca, like the others whom I met, attributed to Sisters Judy, Ann, and Josella, not only the knowledge acquired, but also and especially, the courage to use that knowledge. I heard over and over again, "She helped me to believe in myself."

The Ann to whom they referred is Ann Kernen, SCN, who succeeded Judy Raley as director of lay ministry in Cayo when the latter was called to community service at Nazareth in 1984. Talking with the women of whom Judy had spoken in her homily and hearing them speak of Judy and Ann was a study in continuity. It was obvious that neither Judy nor Ann had tried to impose a style or method of ministry. Both of them had observed how Francisca, Bernadine, Neya, Ycela, Teody, Maria, and all the others were inclined to act and had encouraged them to use their natural gifts and the grace of their ministry. Josella was still assisting them in a similar manner when I last visited there.

San Ignacio is truly Belizean, but, like every other area of Belize, it has its own distinctive character—people, language, customs—that

SCN Ann Kernen, in the center of this group of three, is hosting, in San Ignacio, SCN Provincial Maria Vincent Brocato and a visitor from India, Olive Pinto, SCN, who is wearing a sari—her native dress. From this snapshot, it is easy to see that the Cayo District is truly hill country. The church in the background is itself built on high ground, but note that its two towers are only slightly higher than the heads of the three strollers on a neighboring hillside.

identifies it specifically. English is the medium in the schools, as it is throughout Belize, but many of the people in the Cayo District, where San Ignacio is located, speak Spanish also. Use of the Spanish language is not surprising, because the district, especially the town of San Ignacio, is close to the Guatemalan border. Many of the older people have come from Guatemala. As is frequently the case, customs are related to language, and vice versa. Ann shares her experience of one of those customs in her account of the nine-day preparation for Christmas, the traditional *Posada*.

This custom, Ann explains, dates from the seventeenth century. It commemorates the journey of Joseph and Mary to Bethlehem and their search for a place to stay. Beginning December 16, each night until Christmas a different house is offered as the dwelling—the *Posada*. The procession begins with children carrying statues of Mary, Joseph, and an angel. A donkey trots along, reminding us that Mary really did ride on one of that animal's ancestors. The people follow, carrying candles and singing, *"Caminando va José"* ("See the father Joseph walking") until they reach the closed doors of the chosen house. Outside the closed doors the group stops and asks in song for lodging.

Ann recalls one particular Christmas season when SCN President Dorothy MacDougall was visiting her and Elizabeth Miles, OP, the San Ignacio local community at the time.

"It was pouring rain," says Ann, "as we joined the *Posada* procession, umbrella in one hand and a song paper and dripping candle in the other. The path was full of potholes that had quickly filled with water. In the darkness I think I stepped in each one, splashing the person in front of me." The song, *"Andan por esos caminos llerosos y fatigados,"* Ann assures us, "took on special meaning as we wended our way" ("So fatigued, they only stumble blindly o'er the darkened way").

The procession begins each night with children carrying statues of Mary and Joseph and an angel . . . .

The people follow, carrying candles. When they reach the posada—the house chosen for the night's celebration—how eagerly they accept the invitation to come inside and rest.

SCN Dorothy MacDougall stops on the porch to observe the musicians who play the marimba vigorously and long. This instrument, like a very long xylophone, is a favorite in Belize.

Finally we reached the house chosen for the *Posada* that night. How eagerly we accepted the invitation to come inside and rest! The melodious marimba on the porch, the fervent prayers, sometimes quite long, the delicious refreshments and, above all, the gracious and joyous camaraderie gave special meaning to that Christmas in Cayo.

After that preparation, so full and so intense, observers may question, "What is left for Christmas day?" The answer is found in every household in Cayo and along the streets and lanes of every town and village. Christmas is a day of family celebration. Below we see Ann visiting a mother and her children and some of the children's friends.

When the sisters visited homes at Christmas time, lay ministers often accompanied them. Those ministers frequently made their own visits, however. Concern for their neighbors was part of their life. One of them, Francisca Jones, speaks of how much it meant to have the sisters encourage them, assuring them of the value of those simple visits. The sisters were not the only ones who encouraged them.

Francesca had spoken, also, of Father Richard, who had encouraged her to invite people to Mass at the Monastery. Richard Walz, OSB, is Prior of Santa Familia, the Benedictine monastery that, in 1996, celebrated the twenty-fifth anniversary of its opening in Cayo. Even though the Benedictines, like the Sisters of Charity, have come to Belize somewhat recently, they trace their heritage, as do all Benedictines, to the foundation by Benedict of Nursia, Italy, in the fifth century. It is customary, however, that a new foundation be made by monks from a monastery within reasonable distance from the site of the new one. The immediate parent of Santa Familia is Subiaco Abbey in Arkansas, USA.

Benedict, would, I am sure, feel immediately at home at Santa Familia. The secret of Benedictine continuity must be the ability to change with the times while maintaining the original spirit, never getting hung up on the characteristics of any particular era.

One time during the eighties when I was living in Belize, I made a private retreat at Santa Familia. I followed the Benedictine horarium for a week, an experience I'll always remember, a memory that I treasure. I occupied a guest room and had all the privacy of a guest. Nevertheless I was also free to join the community of five, as I chose to do, for prayer and meals. Sometimes at dinner there was reading from the original rule, sometimes there was recreation (conversation). After meals I helped to dry the dishes that Brother Jésus washed in a very large sink.

As I sat on the porch or roamed about the fields, reflecting on the Rule that Benedict had written in the fifth century, I marveled at how well it applies to us at the beginning of the twenty-first, in spite of some of Benedict's comments that reveal differences so great as to be amusing. Evidently, it was not always easy, in those days, to check biographical background of some of the men who applied for membership. As a result, some rather unusual characters entered the monastery, at least briefly.

One afternoon the telescoping of centuries brought Benedict so close that I recognized him as director of my retreat. I could not resist putting to him in reverie a question that had been pursuing me all day. He was amused, I think, but in a kindly way, when I said:

Benedict, they call you founder and abbot,
    I find you prophet.
They tell startling miracles of you,
    I find the greatest miracle of all
    your spirit, your way of life, intact
    after a millennium and a half here in Belize.
Today, when vowed life is threatened,
    you say to me,
"Within the freedom of God's children
    basic discipline must reside,
    until the human heart becomes
    immersed so deeply
    in love of God
    values all are in that target centered."
I ask, "Can we recapture discipline that once we had,
    yet keep the spirit of freedom so lately found?"
And you reply, "I've watched Benedictines do it
    now and again throughout the centuries."
"But how?" I ask.
Benedict only smiles, a knowing twinkle in his eye.
He knows I know the answer,
and what we're in for if we try.

Some friends with whom I have shared this little "interview" with Benedict have seemed surprised. They ask, "Do you think we'll go back to the old way of living community life?" My response is, "Of course not. The old way is past; it was good for those times, but I am confident that there are new ways coming. They are already here in embryo. We just don't recognize them. We need to be alert, aware of the trends, for we have a responsibility to help those trends to become a reality."

The souvenir of the silver jubilee celebration of the monastery is a booklet entitled *The Benedictine Presence in Belize*. It consists

almost entirely of excerpts from letters between Santa Familia in
Belize and Subiaco in Arkansas. It is a delightful account of the ups
and downs encountered in a new beginning of an ancient way of life.

That ancient way is reflected in an ongoing life of prayer and
work and of reaching out to the needs of the people nearby. Gradually that reaching out has extended in some ways to the entire country. For example, in response to many requests and with financial
assistance from various sources, the monks have built a retreat center that accommodates eighteen retreatants. The place, called St.
Benedict's Center, is well used, not only for retreats, but also for
meetings of groups of teachers, diocesan organizations, religious
communities, including the Sisters of Charity of Nazareth, as well as
a group of scientists studying the ancient civilization of the area.

An excerpt from a 1995 letter states:

> Knocking on the door as the priests' retreat was drawing to a
> close was Anabel Ford and her troop of archeologists from the
> University of California at Santa Barbara. They are doing basic
> research on the Mayans who lived in a ceremonial center
> about twelve miles from here.

The souvenir booklet in which that letter is quoted gives a heartening account of the growth of that monastery from very bleak begin-
nings twenty-five years earlier. Among dozens of other interesting
items in that booklet is one of special interest to SCNs. It states:

> We marveled at many events in connection with the profession
> of Brother Julio on August 15. A special visitor was Sister
> Paschal Fernicola. She works in the villages where Brothers
> Marcos and Julio are from and made the difficult trip to be
> here. It meant a lot to both young men and to Sister Paschal
> as well.

The Benedictines came to Belize three years before the SCNs.
They had, of course, been preceded many years earlier by the Jesuits,
the Sisters of Mercy, the Sisters of the Holy Family, and the Pallottine
Sisters. It was the latter who hosted me so cordially in Cayo during

my visit in 1997, and it was during that visit that I learned something of their history, especially of their early history in Belize. They came from Germany in 1913, a genuine missionary community. Founded by Vincent Pallotti in 1835, the Pallottines are today in Brazil, Poland, Rwanda, the Ukraine, England, Tanzania, South Africa, India, Switzerland, the United States, and Belize. Their motherhouse, originally in Germany, is now in Rome.

Most people who have spent a little time in Belize know of the shipwreck in 1923 that took the life of Bishop Frederick Hopkins. Many are surprised, however, to learn that two Pallottines, Mary Francesca, superior of the American foundation, and Mary Vincent, the newly elected Belizean superior, also died in that accident. Barely escaping with her life was the general of the Order, Mother Mary Cecilia. Those sacrifices provided a firm foundation for the building of a strong Pallottine presence in Belize. They have ministered throughout Belize, from Corozal in the north to Toledo in the south, teaching in elementary schools, including at least one that serves

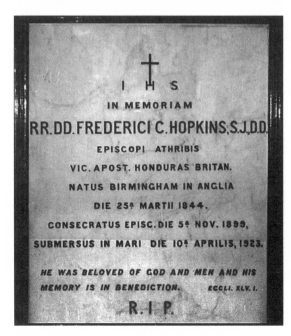

Bishop Hopkins's body is entombed in the Cathedral in Belize City. The memorial on the wall there states that he was drowned. It does not mention that he gave up his seat in a rescue boat to a mother with a child.

severely handicapped students. They teach in high schools; the very large Pallotti High School is a prominent landmark in the center of Belize City. Staying with those sisters in Cayo during Holy Week and Easter in 1997, I was often reminded of the days a decade earlier when SCNs Ann Kernen and Paschal Maria Fernicola had been active in ministry there. Paschal had joined Ann when Elizabeth Miles left Cayo to join Ransom in Belize City; Ann Kernen and Paschal continued to minister there for three years.

When the SCNs left Cayo in 1988, Ann wrote for *SCNews,* "It is a well known fact that the missioners' purpose in any land is to enable the people with whom they have worked to assume leadership and to move on their own as soon as it is feasible."

When Ann accompanied Elizabeth to Belize City, they stopped for a visit at St. Catherine's Academy, seen in the background. (See the story of the Academy in Chapter Thirteen.)

Chapter Seven

REFLECTION
IN THE HILLS OF CAYO

Whenever I go to Belize, two places in Cayo draw me like magic—the front porch of the house that used to be the SCN residence there and the ruins of the Mayan temple, Xunantunich, eight miles down the Western Highway. Despite my tight schedule when I visited Belize in 1997, I succumbed to the temptation to spend a few hours in each place.

There is magic in the sea, but Cayo's hills have a charm all their own. My first experience of those hills occurred one Christmas season in the early eighties, just a few years after SCNs Judy Raley and Kitty Wilson had opened the SCN house there in 1978. I took the Batty Bus to downtown San Ignacio. (For the enlightenment of those who might be smiling at the bus title, Batty is a highly respected family name in that area, having nothing of the connotation implied in the United States.) After leaving the bus, I climbed the steep, rocky road up to the SCN house at the top of what seemed to me a minor mountain. It is worth the climb. The view from the porch is breathtaking. The town of San Ignacio below seems to be the flowering of roots planted deep in the "mountain side."

When I returned there in 1997, the house looked just as it had looked fifteen years earlier. If it was occupied, the occupants were not at home. No one disturbed me.

Seated on the porch at sunset, recalling the earlier experience, I felt rather than saw the warm colors melt into the darkness. Gradually lights come on in the houses and memory reminded me that at that other time the lights had been mostly red and green, as it was Christmastime. Now, closing my eyes, I felt briefly a part of the scene once more, just as if I had become a figure in a painting. Soon, however, I was brought back to reality, reassured by paths of street lights that seemed to direct car lights along steep, curving roads.

One center of activity soon loomed large at the foot of the hill. Traffic was slowing down there, and I recalled how, in the past, cars would line up, their drivers awaiting turns to drive across the one-lane Hawkesworth Bridge over the Macal River into the town on the other side. That town is Santa Elena, smaller and less busy than San Ignacio, but from the porch at the top of the hill, it appeared to be simply a mirrored reflection of the larger town. At least that is the way it seemed to me both times that I visited San Ignacio.

One SCN, who graciously agreed to read this account, tells me "there weren't that many cars in Cayo fifteen years ago." I want to accept the comment of an experienced resident, but I know I didn't create that memory. I tell myself that it doesn't take a great number of cars to cause a bottleneck. Besides, now, fifteen years later, there are two bridges there to handle the traffic. That says something.

Dramatic change has taken place through the years. One of the Pallottine sisters there told me recently that when she was very young, sixty-five years ago, the sisters in San Ignacio and Santa Elena seldom saw sisters from other houses in their community, so difficult was travel in those days. "There were really very few roads," she said, "and they were practically impassable." San Ignacio would host a retreat one year and Santa Elena would attend. The following year Santa Elena would host the retreat and San Ignacio would attend. They followed the same plan for social get-togethers. The isolation was real, but the area was a beautiful one in which to be isolated.

Like the little house at the top of the hill that seemed to be seated on a mountain, the highest temple at Xunantunich rests atop another of Cayo's massive hills. The rocks that form that hill have,

The Hawkesworth Bridge is ordinarily crowded with cars and trucks. On the day of this picture, it was cleared for pedestrians so that marchers welcoming the new bishop could cross safely.

for more than a thousand years, been sunk deep into firm black ground. A little stream running parallel to the highway would obscure the road to the temple were it not for a faithful rustic ferry that always stands ready to take the visitor across. Sometimes there is a long line of cars awaiting transportation. When I visited there in 1997, I was the only visitor at nine o'clock one morning, so I didn't have to wait in the usual line.

The man who controlled the cable that pulled me across required that I get out of the car "for safety's sake" for the duration of the five-minute journey. There is no charge for that journey; it is considered a part of the road. As we touched land, I got back into the car, drove off the ferry and up the steep mud road. It was a beautiful drive through a veritable forest of overhanging trees, penetrated here and there by a shaft of sunlight. I soon reached a stretch of level ground and rolled into a designated parking space.

A little stream running parallel to the highway would obscure the road to the ruin were it not for the faithful rustic ferry that always stands ready to take the visitor across.

Just a few steps ahead and to the right as one enters the compound, sits a contemporary log cabin, much like those found in parks in the United States. The hospitality one experiences when being welcomed by Elfego Panti, the caretaker, is enhanced by his sharing of information about the Maya people. A Mayan himself, he has spent a lifetime learning as much as possible about his ancestors.

The name Xunantunich (The "X" is sounded like a cross between an "s" and a "z") means in English "Maiden of the Rock" or "Stone Woman." At the very center of several plazas is the monolith El Castillo—massive but well proportioned and graceful. That anything so massive can be so graceful is proof of the Mayan gift of mathematical skill. Throughout the plazas, chiefly at the bases of stairways, very large faces are carved in the stone slabs. A stroll through the ancient monument teases the imagination. Some places, however, are well identified; for example, the ball-court. The guide and the published literature explain that the games played there were significant. The winners, of course, were honored, as would be expected. The members of the losing team, however, were put to death! We are told, nevertheless, that they went gladly, for they were considered heroes!

One wonders about the Mayan interpretation of eternal life. For example, children were sacrificed to the gods. Surely any parent who witnessed the sacrifice of a child to a god at the pinnacle of the temple must have believed that that child was with the gods.

Of the hundreds of such sites in Belize, many are in various stages of excavation. Archaeologists have been working spasmodically at Xunantunich since 1894, seriously since 1938. Mahler and Wotkyns, authors of *Belize a Natural Destination,* pp. 228-231, write that the tallest structures were not stabilized until 1960. The authors support the theory that the site once suffered a severe earthquake. The importance of central stabilization is evident. Should El Castillo, 135 feet high, not be stable, the result could be disastrous.

The ancient Maya, famous for their knowledge of mathematics, made ascending the rock relatively pleasant, so well proportioned are the slant and depth of the steps. The temple at the top of El Castillo, old as it is, is not the first one built there. Rather it is the last one built before the mysterious disappearance of the Maya, sometime before the end of the first millennium. There, as elsewhere in Maya lands, excavations have revealed a series of temples built one on top of the other. At the pinnacle, one can look across the border into the green fields of Guatemala and down upon three plazas of Xunantunich, an unforgettable panorama.

Memories of that view from former visits re-enforced the ever-present temptation to scale the rock one more time. That day of my last journey to the ancient ruin was not a time for exploration, however. It was, rather, a time for recalling people and events of nearly twenty years. The place had always offered me an ideal atmosphere for recollection, something for which I felt the need. I had come back to Belize to refresh my memory about much that I had known and experienced during my six-year residence there in the eighties. After visiting many places that I knew and talking with old friends, I had moved on to become better acquainted with parts of the country that

I had visited during those years but in which I had not resided. I had come to try to piece together the history that I had learned from reading annals, from talking with SCNs, SCNAs, and others who had been in ministry there, some briefly, others for a number of years.

Two months had not been long enough to absorb all that I was experiencing, but I had to bring my visit to a close in order to go home to try to record something of that experience. Actually, I had wanted to develop more than a record; I had hoped to share with those who would read it something of the rich reality of the land and people of Belize.

I closed my eyes and, imagining that I was surrounded by Mayas of a thousand years ago, I wondered how they would answer some of the questions surfacing in my mind. The theologian Karl Rahner, SJ, believed that those who have gone before us are all around us. That we are unable to communicate with them, he said, is our limitation, not theirs. Had the spirits of those first Belizeans observed, during the Middle Ages, the coming of the various groups of Europeans, they would have learned from them about the effect of Christianity on the world, especially on their homeland. They would have witnessed the coming of many people from Mexico during the War of the Castes, people who were Catholic, whatever might have been their education in the Faith. They would have seen how, in recent years, missionaries from England and the United States had brought both faith and education. Had they followed the history to that point, they would understand my questions. First, however, I would have to form those questions.

That day it seemed to me that the all-encompassing question was: as we consider twenty-five years in Belize, what is the place of the SCNs here? In attempting an answer, I am influenced by other questions and comments that I hear occasionally: (1) We went to Belize to assist a pastor in a parish and found ourselves involved in the development of lay ministry. We did that to the extent that lay ministers may function. Should we, then, consider our task accomplished and withdraw? (2) While we were helping to develop the Lay Ministry Program, we became involved in the development of other projects, such as the Child Development Center; the new parish, St. John Vianney; and residences that enable young women from remote areas to attend high school. Then SCNs from both India and the United States contributed to much needed health care in Belize for a number of years. The new parish and the child-development center are doing well without our presence in either one of them. Should that remind us that part of the mission of men and women religious is to encourage the laity to assume responsibility for ministry? (3) On the other hand, although SCN/As have succeeded in the ministry to which they were called in Belize originally, has not their experience there directed them to still other ministries?

Those of us who have been in many villages and who have talked with knowledgeable people about health, education, and other important aspects of life know that the needs continue to be very great. To identify some of those needs, we have only to take note of some of the interviews that we have recorded: Superintendent Clement Wade's describing the need for more well-prepared teachers of religion in the Catholic schools; Health Education Director Anthony Nicasio's pointing out the need for health education of mothers in many villages, education that could be offered by teachers prepared to teach health in the elementary school; and Phyllis and Roy Cayetano's explaining the need for teachers of the arts in the elementary school. These are only a few of the needs revealed in various ways throughout this book. The work of the Cayetanos—cultural leaders in Dangriga—is more thoroughly treated in Chapter Eight.

Pondering contemporary needs that morning at Xunantunich, as I sat on the steps of El Castillo, I wondered what had been the needs of the great Maya civilization. What might have been done to preserve that civilization? What would be their advice to us today with regard to the multiethnic people of Belize, their gifts and their needs?

The sun was making its way through my hat, reminding me that the time for reflection was over. Visitors were beginning the long climb up El Castillo. Families, individuals, one school group with the teacher reminding the students to look for certain characteristics, broke the silence of my Maya morning. It was a welcome break,

At the very center of several plazas is the monolith El Castillo, massive but well proportioned and graceful. That anything so massive can be so graceful is proof of the Mayan gift of mathematical skill. Proof of that skill also is the ease with which one can reach the top.

however, bringing together once again the ancient world and the world of today.

Since that day at Xunantunich our congregation has established a central house in Belize City, indicating confidence in our call to minister in Belize. At this writing there are six SCNs in Belize City, but there is promise of several planning to join them. At present, we have consolidated our mission by having one local community in Belize City and by working out from there to the Stann Creek District. The promise of others coming suggests houses elsewhere. Perhaps that promise may be fulfilled by the time this account is published.

As SCNs assembled in Dangriga in the Jubilee Year 2000 to celebrate twenty-five years of Belize-SCN/A relationship, I was moved to pray, *"O God, the harvest is great indeed but the laborers far too few."*

Chapter Eight

STANN CREEK DISTRICT IN INDEPENDENT BELIZE

Belize was on the threshold of independence when Sarah Ferriell, SCN, took up residence in Dangriga late in the summer of 1981. Mary Lynn Fields, SCN, had been called to Belize City to initiate the Lay Ministry Program there, and Sarah had volunteered to take her place in the Stann Creek District.

By that time the program had been firmly established in Dangriga. Many faithful ministers from the villages also came frequently to Dangriga for meetings, classes, and workshops. Considering the roads and methods of travel at that time, those ministers made genuine efforts to remain faithful. The greatest number of ministers in any one village, however, was six; a number of the villages had only one each.

Sarah saw, therefore, the need to spend time in the villages on the Southern Highway. In each one of them she set up a Bible School and a program for ministry training. She stayed in each place for whatever length of time seemed necessary to get the project moving. Sometimes it was a night or two, sometimes one or two weeks. Fond memories of those sessions were recounted for me in 1993 by some of the ministers who had attended them.

By the time Sarah arrived in Dangriga, Mike Oliver, SJ, whose call for help in Sacred Heart parish had triggered the whole ministry movement in Belize, had been transferred to San Antonio. Jim Short,

SJ, who had responded to Mike, had completed his term as Jesuit superior and was succeeding Mike as pastor in Dangriga. Jim had not yet come when Sarah arrived, so she made those first visits to the villages unannounced.

When she arrived in Hopkins, Sarah greeted those who welcomed her, introduced herself, and explained that Father Short would not be there that day. With that, a voice from the group responded, "Sis, you will be our priest today."

Sarah learned that the voice was Marcella Lewis's and that Marcella was indeed a well-known lay minister, a gifted Belizean woman, "one to write a book about." In fact, there is a small volume about her. Sarah was to learn also that she would often be called "Sis," a term of endearment for sisters among the Garifuna and Creole people. That one greeting by Marcella was a perfect welcome for Sarah. From that moment she was Sis to many people in the villages and in Dangriga.

To review the early attendance lists from the villages is to hear echoes of familiar names. There is Georgetown with Garcia, Martinez, and Lopez; Maya Center with Bolon and Saqui; Mango Creek with Longsworth, Ciego, and Lambey. There is Chun in Maya-Mopan, Ching and Sho in Santa Rosa, Flores in Seine Bight, Lambey in Middlesex, Villanueva in Whoa Leaf. Many of those names are found also in lists from San Roman, Pamona, South Stann Creek, and Independence.

Returning to Dangriga from the villages, Sarah was greeted by Father Short, who had arrived during her get-acquainted visit to the villages. Jim has a wealth of stories about those days. To enjoy them fully, it is necessary to recall their setting, the church-school-rectory compound that is Sacred Heart, Dangriga. For the reader who has not yet visited Dangriga, the next best thing is to picture the church facing the sea, and the school, a low, rambling building, to the north. On the side street to the south, but still in the compound, stands the rectory, a two-story structure with trees here and there in the yard. Near it are parked a car and a truck with signs of work being done on both of them, as with most cars and trucks that travel Belizean roads. Jim tells of approaching the truck one day and finding Ijo, one of the occasional workmen, already settled in it, awaiting the "chauffeur." This dialog followed:

"Come on out, Ijo."

"Go with you."

"No, not now."

"You only stingy, Fada!"

Then there was Sup (pronounced soop), Jim's nickname for the janitor, whose real name was Portelino Vicenti and who came from Seine Bight. The nickname was short for superior. Sup visited the villages by boat where, according to Jim, he often became "bishop."

Jim says that Sup was exceedingly slow but that he possessed a powerful personality, by which he was able to draw the whole community together. He was anything but presentable; yet when he served Mass, which he did frequently and well, his unfailing pleasantness outweighed his lack of cleanliness even at the sharing of peace.

Among those stories is one about the day when Jim, having just closed the church after the six o'clock morning Mass, met a woman holding a little boy by the hand. Evidently she had told the child that the church was God's house. When, therefore, their paths and Jim's crossed, the logical little boy called out, "Mornin' God."

Jim recalls encounters with many unusual people; for example, Ian Roman, the blind tailor, who had undergone surgery many times. One of those times, when Father sympathized with him, his response was: "Don't worry, Father. Every time they cut on me God loves me more."

Although there are many stories that are a joy to record, there are some that are painfully sad. Edelberto Conti was a highly respected lay minister, a devoted family man. He taught his daughters to read Scripture, not only at home but also in church, an unusual ministry for the Ketchi women. Unlike many people in that area at that time, he recognized individuals as persons rather than as representatives of a particular gender. He was deeply aware of his daughters' value.

The sister of Edelberto's wife lived on the edge of the village with her husband Profilio. The latter jealously suspected Edelberto of having relations with his wife. As a result Profilio killed Edelberto. A tragedy for both families! That Jim recalls those stories, some with humor and others with sadness, is evidence of how close to the people the church of the eighties in Dangriga really was.

Fifteen years later, when I visited Dangriga, Nunce Miguel, a lay minister there, recalled those early days when she had worked with Sarah. She told of how hesitant she had been to do all that the ministry required.

"But Sister Sarah helped me as I became a Eucharistic Minister and a Reader," Nunce said; "Sister Sarah helped us come closer to ourselves." That seemed to mean "to have confidence in ourselves." By way of illustration Nunce recalled, with special pleasure, going to Maya Center caroling at Christmas time.

Nunce is realistic, however. She recognizes all that is needed to keep the ministry program alive. She mentioned the villages that continue to send representatives to the meetings and "those that need to be renewed." She pointed out that Dennis Martinez, whose name is on the original list from Seine Bight, is now president of the Lay Ministers. Another minister from that early group is Philip Nicasio, to whom Nunce gives credit for doing quietly many things that must be done but who receives little notice.

Nunce expressed great expectations with regard to Loraine Gomez, a member of the faculty of St. John's College, who is director of the Lay Ministry Program for the entire country. She calls her a dynamic woman, a description borne out by an article in the *Christian Herald* for October 1997. Written by Loraine herself, that article announces the election of "two vital bodies" to direct the Lay Ministry Program of Belize. Loraine, with the assistance of Dennis, Phillip, and other dedicated ministers, promises the "new life" called for by Nunce.

Nunce Miguel (now Olivia Bregal) and SCN Sarah Ferriell share a reading at the Jubilee Liturgy. Nunce is typical of Belizean faithfulness. Whether timidly becoming a minister in the late seventies or recognizing the need for renewal of the Program in the nineties or celebrating its maturity in 2000, she is always there.

While new life is certainly needed in many places, some of the original groups have never slackened their pace. The ongoing ministry of the "founding group" in Dangriga, the very first Belizean Ministers of the Word, is an example of that continuity, as will be seen in Chapter Twenty.

Nunce says, "I get discouraged but find myself keeping on." Discouraged but keeping on would seem to be the transition experience of the growth process.

Mae Norales, another faithful Dangriga minister, recalled Sarah Ferriell's strong leadership followed by that of SCNs Adeline Fehribach and Amina Bejos. "Then," she said, "there was a period of letdown." Now, however, she believes the Lay Ministry Program is stabilized.

Mae's most optimistic, enthusiastic statement referred to the public attitude toward government. She said, "Now that our youth are educated, they can no longer be fooled." Revealing her own source of wisdom, she told me that she teaches twenty-three three-year-olds in preschool.

When Sarah Ferriell caught Amina Bejos in quiet action among the children of Seine Bight, she produced one of those pictures worth a thousand words.

Adeline Fehribach addresses the Ministers of the Word in Dangriga.

Juanita and Simeon Joseph, who welcomed me next, are proud to be Belizean, proud to be Garifuna. "Our culture is unique," they told me. That is their message as they speak to me at their home in Dangriga, as well as when they address the SCN Associates at Nazareth, Kentucky.

They always express appreciation of Lynn and of the SCNs generally. They recognize the charism of the SCN community, inherited from the first Sisters of Charity, founded in the seventeenth century by St. Vincent de Paul.

Vincent told those sisters that they would be having "no other monastery than the houses of the sick or the school room; no other cell than a hired room or a poor cabin; no other chapel than the parish church; no other cloister than the public streets." He even told them not to call themselves religious or sisters. "You are rather *daughters* of *charity*," he said. As Cardinal Suenens, speaking at Mundelein College shortly after Vatican II, expressed it, "Vincent was a very smart man. He was afraid that the Church would clap his new community behind bars as it had done the Sisters of the Visitation, founded by Vincent's friend, Francis de Sales, and they would no longer be able to serve the poor."

In the Church of today's world, unlike that of Vincent's day, many other women religious are in very public ministries, and Sisters of Charity do have convents, and chapels within those convents. Since public ministry was written into their original rule, however, when all other women religious were cloistered, or semi-cloistered, that public image is likely to show through at times. Such a time was the beginning of SCN ministry in Belize, and Simeon Joseph recognized it. "Your hearts and doors were open to us," he said. Of the Lay Ministry Program he stated proudly, "My wife was a founding member."

It would be impossible to talk with everyone who could share valuable memories of those early days, and who would gladly do so. Those whom I reached were generous with both their time and their memories, and fortunately there were among them a variety of both memories and opinions.

A conversation with Fabian Cayetano, who holds a government position in Dangriga, summed up for me many aspects of Belizean history, including Belizean Church history. One Sunday morning, after eight o'clock Mass, we sat on the porch that extends the entire length of the second floor of the convent of the Holy Family Sisters. That porch facing the sea is an ideal place for an uninterrupted conversation.

Fabian spoke of the Church, which had recently taken a stand to promote justice for the workers. He described his country as "a young, struggling nation trying to establish itself among older nations." He expressed regret that many television programs originating in the United States were creating a false impression of what is desirable. He was referring especially to the advertising that promises immediate health, wealth, beauty, and anything else the viewer desires.

When I talked with him that day in 1997, Fabian was excited about the planned celebration of the second centenary of the Battle of St. George's Caye when "slave and freeman fought together" to hold the caye against the Spanish. The Garifuna culture, he said, embraces the Amerindian and African, the Carib and the Arawac that came together to form ancestry that embraces language, food, customs, healing, and religious practices.

The last two include the *Dugu*, a kind of healing ceremony. The Garifuna believe that within that ceremony they can communicate with the dead, "thereby tapping into the power of their ancestors." One of the tour books points out that the ritual is "rarely seen by outsiders." By courtesy of the group and its leader, however, this "outsider" and two others were present at one evening's *Dugu*. I was impressed by the serious, respectful, prayerful attitude of every member of the large group. We left after we had, for several hours, observed their slow, rhythmic movement to the accompaniment of chant. In order really to participate, it would be necessary to continue this ritual an entire week. I wonder whether this westerner, with no drop, so far as she knows, of Asian or African blood, could sustain it. (For a recent account see Susie Post Rust's story and photographs in *National Geographic,* September 2001, pp. 102–113.)

It is Fabian's opinion that Garifuna and Mestizo are better at cooperation than are Garifuna and Creole. He is encouraged, however, by the work of the National Creole Council. Tom Barry (*Inside Belize,* p. 68) echoes this estimate. He points out that in spite of the similarity in appearance of the Garifuna and the Creole, "there exists continuing racial animosity between the two groups." Nevertheless, like Fabian, he is encouraged by the work of the Afro/Belizean group founded in Belize City in 1991 "to promote understanding and solidarity." They will surely succeed, for both groups are intelligent, and their animosity nonviolent.

Fabian paid high tribute to the Jesuit educators, particularly their efforts to educate all children, and, especially, in an earlier time, the children of slaves. Methodist missionaries followed the same procedure in Dangriga, he said. He stressed the tremendous contribution toward national improvement made by the Sisters of Mercy, the Pallottine Sisters, and the Holy Family Sisters, all of whom continue to educate children and young adults of Belize. Some of those sisters are also involved in health care and in other types of ministry. He recalled the coming of the Sisters of Charity of Nazareth "with a different approach, the development of lay ministry. That ministry," he pointed out, "had been established by Vatican Council II and thoroughly researched and demonstrated by Elizabeth Wendeln and Ken Williams." Recalling the work of Lynn Fields, he said, "The results of her efforts have grown. The movement now needs a support system." For the record, it is important to recall, as indicated earlier in this chapter, the SCN call to Belize was to assist in a parish. The simultaneous call of the Church for the institution of lay ministry brought the two together. The melding of the two was so immediate and so complete that many people, some SCNs included, have forgotten that the original call was for one sister to assist a pastor in one parish.

Fabian pointed to the growth in the villages encouraged and led by Sarah. "Now," he said, "we see the organization of a National

Board of Directors to align and integrate the Lay Ministry Movement throughout the country." Finally, Fabian spoke of the increasing number of good books on Belize by Belizeans and of their
availability through Angelus Press and the new public library. Some
of those books are listed in the bibliography of this volume.

Just as the porch was a very good place for the interview, it was
ideal for reflection on the insights acquired in that conversation.
After Fabian had left, I sat there, watching a big fishing vessel far out
in the Caribbean, so still that it reminded me of Coleridge's "painted
ship upon a painted ocean." In contrast to Coleridge's ship of "The
Ancient Mariner" that bespoke death, however, the Belizean vessel
reminded me of Fabian's description of his country as "a young,
struggling nation trying to establish itself among older nations." That
vessel, I knew, was anchored at a particular place off the Belizean
shore because that place must be alive with shrimp.

It was the evening of that same Sunday in the spring of 1997 that
I met with Carmella Vargas Castillo. As we talked that night in the
parlor of Holy Family Convent, I recalled the first time that I had met
her in 1980, during my first visit to Belize. She had come to say
"Good-bye" to Lynn, before leaving for Jamaica to prepare to
become a nurse practitioner. She, a registered nurse, and SCN Anna
Marie Nalley, herself a nurse practitioner, had been working together
in Dangriga for some time. Knowing the need for more practitioners,
and recognizing the quality of Carmella's professional service, Anna
Marie had recommended Carmella for study and advancement.

Legend has it that there was hesitation on the part of the administration of the department of health. Carmella was "too outspoken."
But Anna Marie spoke up for Carmella, giving examples of her work
as a professional and as a big-hearted person, compassionate toward
the poor and suffering, especially in the villages. Fortunately, Anna
was listened to, and Carmella became a nurse practitioner.

By the time of my visit with Carmella in 1997, Anna Marie had
returned to the United States, and Carmella had been transferred
from Dangriga to the new village of San Juan. That village had been
set up by the Irish company, Fyffe, to house the workers on its

banana plantation. Many plantation workers at that time were refugees from Guatemala, El Salvador, and Honduras. Without attempting to analyze the situation from a distance, yet listening to responsible people who were near the scene, one can easily see that the conditions in which the workers were living needed improvement. That steps have been taken to bring about that improvement is evident from a conversation with Carmella. The government had employed Carmella as resident nurse practitioner for the village that Fyffe had set up to house its workers. The government had also established a clinic. The company built the houses. Carmella told me that each family was paying a monthly fee that in twenty years will have covered the cost of purchasing the house.

Carmella finds the administration of the village to be very good. She says that Fyffe does not interfere. She is on two committees, housing and discipline. She says that there is no abuse or gambling; drinking is in moderation. The village has its own electrical system; lights are out at ten each night; lamps are used after that. There is no running water from midnight until six a.m. Carmella has electricity until midnight. At the time of a banana shipment, electricity is on around the clock.

In order to illustrate her point about the way the administration works, Carmella told of a man who had had to appear for the third time before the disciplinary committee, of which she is a member. He had had two previous warnings about his approach toward women sexually. The committee found him guilty. He was dismissed, and he cannot be rehired.

Carmella mentioned the many conveniences that the people of the village enjoy, such as weekly garbage collection. Since that interview I have heard that many of the people would like to become Belizean citizens, and they are receiving assistance in preparing to do so. We still hear stories that conflict with Carmella's experience. Some people remember the government's harshness in the beginning of the immigration from other Central-American countries. We continue to hope that the people who left their homelands seeking safety and peace will eventually find what they are seeking in Belize.

The following day when I talked with Sally and Augustine Flores in their home, they recalled their time in Cleveland, Ohio. Augustine had worked at Union Carbide while he was attending Franciscan High School and St. John University. When he finished school, he could have had a very good position, but they both wanted to get back home to Belize and to their families.

One of their interests was the Garifuna Council, founded in 1978. Fabian Cayetano had mentioned the value of the Council in bringing ethnic groups together. Evidence of that characteristic was revealed when Augustine reviewed the number of places in which branches of the Council are found: Corozal, Libertad, Barranco, Belize City, Belmopan, Dangriga, Hopkins, Georgetown, Seine Bight, Punta Gorda. Nor is the organization limited to Belize. Recently, according to Augustine, the groups in Belize have joined with Garifuna groups in Honduras, Nicaragua, Panama, and Costa Rica to form CABO, Central American Black Organization, with headquarters in Lateida, Honduras.

"We hope to educate our people in the value of land and in the necessity of documenting our rights," said Augustine.

"It is important to keep abreast of change in values," said Sally. By way of illustration she added, "Ten years ago this property was worth $585; now it would cost $1,000 to have it surveyed." (It is important to keep in mind that the Belize dollar is equal to half the US dollar.)

Other purposes of the Council, they said, are improvement of the economic and social condition of the people; defense of people suffering from injustices; and general preservation of the culture. They spoke of Phyllis Cayetano and of what she is doing for the arts. Fortunately, I was able to meet Phyllis very soon afterward and to talk with her and her husband Roy, who is currently the president of the National Garifuna Council.

Both of them spoke of art in Belize, called it a "spontaneous outpouring, much of it oral." "Many ethnic groups," they said, "are in transition from oral to written." They spoke of craft, dance, storytelling.

"Some people," they said, "excelled in spite of the school system that until recently did not include art in the curriculum—a tribute to the resilience of the culture." In speaking of art, Roy recalled musicians Benjamin Nicholas (mentioned above in Chapter Two) and Pen Cayetano as recognized internationally, although the latter has only a standard four education officially but is self-educated.

Roy pointed out that for years there was virtually no music education. Musicians just sprang up. Traditionally everybody is a composer. The sounds are made while doing something else. "Music serves," he said, "as a record of happenings, historical events, songs about you and what you've done." Roy also spoke of music as accompaniment for dancing, different kinds of songs being associated with different kinds of dances.

Phyllis pointed out that, unlike much of the dancing for show with which we are familiar, the dancing in Belize is not for show. "There is no dividing line between dancers and spectators. Dancing is for the enjoyment of the participants. People suddenly jump in, sometimes two at a time," she said. When Phyllis started her dance program, *Wari Bagadaga,* the very first groups pulled together quickly. She added reflectively, "Garifuna constitute only seven and one-half percent of the population of Belize, but it is a strong group, and they share generously."

Roy recalled, for example, that Andy Palacio had been very successful the previous summer in Brussels, but that he had also conducted workshops in Belize City, Punta Gorda, Livingston, and Guatemala. "Garifuna have contributed greatly to this country," said Roy. "To survive the first quarter of the new century, however," he maintains, "we need to use the language in daily life. We need Garifuna names for new inventions. Art, music are comments on daily life. We must accommodate to reality."

Phyllis and Roy have done their part toward preserving and promoting their culture, and their enthusiasm is contagious (see Roy quoted in the issue of *National Geographic* referred to above, p. 107). I wondered, however, whether the very young people would take the time, make the effort even to use the *People's Garifuna Dictionary* that Roy has compiled. Of course, as mentioned in the first chapter, there is the current interest in the Garifuna culture in progress at the Field Museum in Chicago, but what about everyday life in Belize?

I soon had an answer to my questions. Gwen Nunez Gonzales, teacher of standard three at Sacred Heart School, is Garifuna, a loyal member of the National Garifuna Council, currently its secretary. She calls the Garifuna culture "rich, unique, God-given." Working on retrieval of the language, she was shocked to learn at a meeting several years ago that only one man knew Garifuna. "Language is the biggest barrier," she said, "as is the attitude of those who haven't spoken it."

Who is this young woman, so eager to keep alive the "rich, unique, God-given culture" of her Garifuna ancestors? Gwen is from Hopkins, where she attended elementary school and where she met SCNs Amina and Adeline. She attended Ecumenical High School in Dangriga, then college in the States.

Hopkins struck a familiar note. "Then you must know Marcella Lewis?" I queried, recalling how Marcella had welcomed Sarah to Hopkins. Gwen's broad smile preceded her hearty "Of course, she's my grandmother."

During our conversation Gwen had mentioned belonging to "Search," the program for youth introduced into Belize by Lynn in the seventies and still enrolling youth of the nineties (See Chapter Five). I was directed to Andrew Chavez to learn more about the present "Search" program. Of course I went gladly, eager to meet another adult who, like Amina and Irene, had, as a youth, experienced "Search."

I found Andrew in his office. He was, at that time, District Manager at the Department of Social Security. Happy to talk about "Search," he started at the beginning of the movement in 1977 when he and several others had gone to Memphis to observe the program there. After a weekend in the States, they had returned to Dangriga to begin the "Search" organization that continues there today. It was started also in Belize City and in Cayo. While it did not continue in the latter two areas, it is now being revived in Belize City at St. Catherine's Academy, as recounted in Chapter Five. Andrew believes that "it is time to look at the program and to revise it according to the needs of today's young people. When we began we did not have to deal with the problems of drugs and gang violence, or the effects of cable television. Moral values have deteriorated." He will find, if he investigates, that Amina and her students have faced those problems. Amina brings her students from Lexington to Nazareth, two hours away, for "Search" retreats. All retreatants at Nazareth's Russell Hall use the same dining room as do the sisters in residence there. At dinner one day recently Amina asked everyone to applaud one of the young men who had just succeeded in "coming clean" of drugs.

Andrew described what the program had meant to him and his fellow high school students. Shortly before our conversation, he and three other alumni had been guests at a dinner at which they had been honored as pioneers. That evening they had told of the value that the program had been in their lives, especially in developing Christian maturity and translating moral values into a way of life. The other honorees were Georgia Flores, now a school principal; Martha Serano, currently studying for the Master's Degree; and Ernesto Saqui, a successful teacher and environmentalist. At that dinner each of the four had made a commitment to send to Ecumenical High School Alumni Association $400 a year for four consecutive years.

Andrew spoke highly of the Social Security Program in Belize, in which he had been very successful since he began working for the department in 1985 after teaching for nine years. He continues his love of teaching, however, going to education meetings whenever he can.

As I left his office, he called to my attention a picture on the wall near the door. It was the framed memorial card from Mary Lynn Fields's Mass of Resurrection, reminding me that the memory of Lynn and her inspiration were still very much alive in Dangriga. The memory of Lynn would certainly be alive in the house that I would visit next, the home of Sylvia Flores, whose mother, Evelyn Avila, had generously prepared the meals for many retreats planned and arranged for by Lynn.

Evelyn remembered Lynn and the retreats, and they were happy memories. By the time of my visit, however, she had aged considerably, and she was very sick that day, too sick for visitors. Telling her that I would return another day, I went into the living room to interview Sylvia. I found her there with a group of students, helping them with homework and the next day's assignments.

When the students had gone and we had settled down for the interview, I learned that Sylvia had spent ten years in New York City. She had studied economics and political science at Hunter College there and is now teaching economics and Spanish at Ecumenical High School in Belize where her daughter is a student.

Since her return to Belize she had served a term as mayor of Dangriga, during which she was able to preserve for recreation and sports the large field opposite the church, school, and convent, when there was a movement to use that land for commercial purposes. Sylvia praised Marciana Funes, who had led the strike against the Fyffe Co. To praise that strike is to present the other side of the story reported in Chapter Four. She mentions that SPEAR (Society for Progress in Education and Research) supported Marciana. Sylvia wants to see groups of women working together, supporting one another, rather than individual women working alone. "There is," she said, "need for a strong women's movement."

Sylvia commented on the high unemployment rate prevalent at that time. When hope was expressed that some of the companies in the process of opening businesses in Belize might improve the employment situation, she said, "We invite companies in, but we do not monitor them sufficiently."

Speaking of Belize having become an independent country, Sylvia recalled how interesting it had been to follow the movement from the vantage point of Hunter College in New York City. She remembered having read an account of the argument in the House of Commons and having had access to old newspapers with letters from people who shared remarkable information gleaned from parents and grandparents.

Sylvia sees much that is needed, much that needs to be done in this new nation. In true Belizean spirit, however, she says, "'Hope springs eternal.' God will step in." As evidence that God has already stepped in, Sylvia pointed out the number of exceptional Belizeans—educators, writers, lawyers, social commentators, and specialists in other fields—who are contributing every day to the development of Belize.

That night, as I filed the notes on my interviews, I told myself that, in order to make my plane the following day, I would have to resist all temptation to add "just one more." It was not easy to keep that resolution, but the file yielded some questionnaires from the United States that had been carefully answered by SCNs and others who had spent summers in Belize. Reading those answers, written at a distance in time and place from the scene itself, brought for me a new dimension in the Dangriga story.

A few of those memories bear telling. Celeste Reedy remembers "the woman who sent us a loaf of warm homemade bread every Saturday . . . the group that got up very early to say 'good-bye' the day we left . . . the little boy who salvaged from the trash can paper written on only one side."

Celeste remembers especially Barbara Flores's profession of vows. "The whole country was involved. People came from great distances. Mass was followed by a full day of celebration." Celeste had been favorably impressed also by a funeral. "The casket," she says, "was placed on the back of a truck and surrounded by members of the family. A long line of friends, relatives, and members of various organizations walked in procession behind the slow-moving truck."

Tom Oates, former President of Spalding University, Louisville, who knows Belize well and who has brought many students from there to the University, has a number of stories. For example, he tells

Celeste remembers especially Barbara Flores's profession of vows. Barbara is the daughter of Jacinta Flores pictured below.

Jacinta Flores, one of the first lay ministers in Dangriga, takes Holy Communion to a sick person in the parish. A younger generation of lay ministers is now following in the footsteps of such pioneers.

of a boy and his father who walked many miles very early one morning to bring him a "going away" present.

Patsy O'Toole, SCNA, a member of the group of high school students from Memphis who had visited Belize in the seventies, remembers with fondness that experience of twenty years ago. She says, "I've been haunted by Belize ever since. It is really true that 'Once you drink the water, you have to keep going back.'" Patsy, now a member of OCA (Office of Congregational Advancement) at Nazareth has been back many times.

Review of the past brings promise of the future. This picture of commissioning at Sacred Heart Church, Dangriga, in 1982 shows Sarah Ferriell (far left) who had recently succeeded Mary Lynn Fields (far right) as director of the Lay Ministry Program in the Stann Creek District.

Commissioning the Ministers is Jack Stochl, SJ, at that time Superior of the Jesuit Community in Belize, assisted by Frank Ring, SJ. New Ministers are from left to right, Sally Flores, (far left) Juanita Joseph (center) and Din Guerrero (right).

Sarah's time in Dangriga and Lynn's move to Belize City had marked a kind of turning point in SCN tenure in Belize. When I returned to Louisville after that rich period of interviews in 1997, I visited Sarah to take her the messages that I had assured her many friends I would deliver immediately. Those messages awakened memories, scattered at first, then focused by my questions. I asked, "What words, what impressions come to mind when I say Belize?"

Sarah reflected, then replied: "Southwater Caye and the coral reef; the full moon rising over the Caribbean; the clear, thundering silence of the star-studded skies." Then she began to fill that setting with people. She remembered the Mayas as "quiet, tribal-minded people living from the land, struggling to keep their culture alive, and the Ketchi, always so hospitable." The Garifuna, she recalled as "proud of being who they are, celebrating annually their history as a people." The Chinese shopkeepers she described as "hardworking, business-minded but extending great warmth, and grateful for any reaching-out to them by the Church."

Sarah also remembered individuals. "There was good, simple Alice Bowman, owner of Pelican Beach Resort; Mario Gonzales, teacher, musician, assertive, reflective artist; Sarah Gongora, woman of deep faith and powerful influence who led the *Dugu* and who preached peace and forgiveness among families. Sarah Gongora died recently.

"Those people had dreams and hopes, not just for themselves, but also for Belize. They follow their dreams and continue to hope," said Sarah, as she recalled those days among the "beautiful variety of shades of humanity, living close to earth, to life, and to death." Then, recalling the famous German economist's book *Small Is Beautiful,* she concluded, "Ernst Schumacher was right, 'small is beautiful.'"

Chapter Nine

JOURNEY FROM KENTUCKY THROUGH MEXICO TO BELIZE

The thermometer hovered near zero the morning of January 20 in 1982 when Mary Lynn Fields and I left Nazareth, Kentucky, for Belize City. At an early Mass on the balcony in the church, Linus Giesler, Chaplain for the Motherhouse, asked God's blessing on our journey. After breakfast, a round of hugs, good wishes, and sound advice from Dorothy MacDougall, SCN President, and a band of other early risers, we set out in a new Ford Courier that would serve us well for the next few years. We spent the first night, January 20, in Little Rock, Arkansas, where SCNs Carole Kaucic, Janice Downs, and Marge Hines welcomed us warmly, not only heart-wise but also weather-wise. Despite the hospitality, however, we took off before sunrise the next morning in order to make it to Texas by nightfall, stopping only long enough to "wave" to SCNs Margaret Vincent Blandford, Joseph Marita Wheatley, Mary Angelita Coomes, and Martha Borders at one of our other Little Rock houses.

Actually night had fallen several hours before we arrived in Mercedes, Texas, but it was still Tuesday. We had promised the folks at Nazareth that we would not drive at night in Mexico, but we had made no promises about night driving in the United States.

The reasons for driving instead of flying to Belize were to have a vehicle for use on the mission and to take with us both household and office equipment. Those practical reasons formed a good excuse for a delightful journey. Because we had not yet settled in Belize City, there was not the usual urgency to get home to take care of unfinished business, so we could enjoy an almost carefree week.

Although Lynn had never lived in Belize City, she had had seven years of experience in Dangriga, and she had made the trip by land from Kentucky to Belize before. I was a complete neophyte. We had set out from Little Rock, determined to reach Mercedes, Texas, before midnight. We drove carefully, observing the speed limit, but almost non-stop. We took turns eating the lunch prepared by our Little Rock hostesses. We even managed alternate afternoon naps. The road was good, traffic minimal except at rush hour, and the weather conducive to both pleasure and safety.

We pulled into Mercedes at midnight and called the SCNs, who were expecting us. They gave us directions to their home. It was easy to find, and the welcome awaiting us from SCNs Carol Ann Messina, Mildred McGovern, and Rosemarie Kirwan was well worth the effort to make it that night. It was not long, however, before sleep took over.

At breakfast, Lynn explained that our eagerness to arrive the previous night was the result of what she had learned on former trips. She recalled that it had proved wise to carry bottled drinking water and juices on a journey through Mexico. Then wisdom had prompted the use of current maps obtained just this side of the border. Finally, after the busy days of preparation and departure recently experienced at Nazareth, it would be well to have a really restful day before continuing the journey.

Interspersed with preparations were visits to the places where our hosts were in ministry—Carol Ann, at the Center of the Farm Workers Union led by Cesar Chavez; Rosemarie, in the large public school where she was the head librarian; and Mildred, in the Office of Communications for the Diocese of Brownsville.

At eleven-thirty our hosts took us to the shrine of Our Lady of San Juan where we had a taste of liturgy in Spanish. After Mass, we joined a group receiving the blessing of pilgrims, and then went outside for the blessing of cars and trucks. The celebrant was a priest of the order of Oblates of Mary Immaculate, well known to the group as JR. He blessed our truck last and gave us the collection of offerings he had received from the other pilgrims. Afterwards there was lunch in a little Mexican restaurant.

In the evening the Raymondville SCNs—Mary Margaret "Maggie" Cooper, Evelyn Fugazzi, and Jane Mary Dickman—came over for dinner. We enjoyed a beautiful community evening that closed spontaneously with prayer.

The next day the bottled water and fruit juice were secured and lodged in carry-on thermos bags, ready to be placed under the seat in the truck at departure time. A well directed tour of downtown Brownsville led to a store where multiple maps were on display. Manifest authority was evident in the maps, and entertaining commentary filled the margins. The original editor of the series of maps had been one of the victims of the Depression in the States in the thirties. Discouraged, he had gone south of the border, where he had set up a fruit stand to support himself and his family. Not only was the sale of fruit successful, but the commentaries on events and on the fruit that he dispensed proved to be even more successful. Thus was born a thriving publishing business, featuring chiefly maps guaranteed "to get you to your destination while entertaining you en route and saving you money as you go."

Those two purposes achieved, we spent the rest of the day in chatting with Carol Ann, Mildred, and Rosemarie, meeting their friends, and learning about their ministries. Carol Ann's stories were especially interesting. *Seeking justice for the farm workers,* under the leadership of Cesar Chavez, was no small enterprise. Carol Ann loved the work. Her ministry there, however, would soon be cut very short by serious illness from which she did not recover. Early the next morning, Thursday, after prayers for a safe and successful journey, a hearty breakfast, and another round of hugs, well wishes, and bits of advice for the road, we drove out of Brownsville, Texas, into Matamoros, Mexico. Since our emigration papers had been carefully filled out, with assistance from experienced friends of the SCNs, there was no delay. In moments we were on our way, waving our gratitude to those whom we had left on the other side of the border.

The road was good, but it was a two-lane highway. We were prepared for that, and we had also been assured that the drivers we would meet were veterans who had long ago worked out a plan. Whenever a driver wanted to pass the car immediately ahead, that driver merely flashed lights wildly, and the driver coming in the opposite direction would slow down and yield the necessary space. Unbelievable? Perhaps, but it really worked. Evidently drivers had agreed that it was the only way to stay alive and get to one's destination. That was 1982. Today, a four-lane highway is probably in place.

Recalling that journey twenty years later, I am tempted to use the old cliché "It seems like yesterday." Being a realist, I find that a cliché like that brings out the skeptic in me. How could twenty times three hundred sixty-five possibly seem like one?

Today as I write and remember and write again, I have to swallow my skepticism and say, "I don't know how; I just know that it does." For a little while I am with Lynn in a little Ford Courier on a two-lane highway in Mexico headed for Belize. For the most part, it is a beautiful journey. We know that the Gulf is to the left of us, and occasionally the road curves in that direction, giving us a glimpse of water sparkling in the sunlight.

Many roads branch off to the right of the highway with signs tempting drivers to turn toward famous old towns and ruins and countless other treasures. Keeping our destination ever in mind, and knowing that taking much time out to explore those treasures would make us late for arrival in Belize and cause concern for our safety, we resisted. If that journey were taking place today, we would surely be calling both Nazareth and Belize City every night to say, "All is well." At that time, however, and under those circumstances, making such telephone calls was less successful than it is today.

We stayed four nights in Mexico, the first in Tampico, the second in Veracruz, the third in Villahermosa, the fourth in Merida. In each of the first three, referring to the information in our maps made it easy to find a good hotel with a safe garage for the truck. Not only was it necessary that the truck itself be safe, but also that its contents be protected. Packed into it were a variety of things that we would need in the house that awaited us at St. Ignatius Parish in Belize City.

Saturday evening we stayed in Tampico at the Impala Hotel and lodged the Courier in the hotel garage. Early Sunday morning we walked about two blocks to the Cathedral Square, a beautiful place brightly lighted in the dark of early morning. In the Cathedral we shared with a very pastoral bishop and a very devout congregation the Liturgy of the Third Sunday of Ordinary Time. Their leaflet missal contained the entire liturgy—Ordinary and Proper—in Spanish, so these two neophyte Hispanics could pray every word with them. After breakfast we continued our journey southward.

Sunday was a beautiful day, mostly sunny with a few light showers now and then. About four in the afternoon the sun and the showers formed a rainbow that seemed to stretch over the Gulf to our left and up into the Sierra Madre Mountains on our right. It was breathtaking. Lynn, who was driving, pulled to the side of the road where we sat silently for a little while, reflecting on what seemed to be the blessing of God on the week just passed and on the one just beginning.

We arrived at the Colonial Hotel in Veracruz about seven in the evening, put the Courier in the hotel garage, and went about finding a bite to eat. Stepping out a hotel door, we found ourselves in the town square where a fiesta was in progress—a band playing, lovers walking arm in arm, children laughing, families enjoying Sunday evening together. We had supper in a little sidewalk cafe, participating in the joy that was all around us.

Our next stop was Villahermosa. Our map recommended the town and showed a direct road from there to Chetumal, the last stop before crossing the border into Belize. True to the recommendation, Villahermosa offered good accommodations for us and for the truck.

We left the hotel at nine the next morning, heading for Merida in the Yucatan, where we arrived about five in the afternoon, obtained lodging in a very reasonable motel, because hotel rooms were not available. We parked the truck immediately below our window and took turns checking on it during the night. Somehow, recalling that "night-watch" and the experiences of the following day breaks the spell of "seeming like yesterday." That Wednesday morning in January 1982 when we left Merida and set out for Chetumal seems a very long time ago.

Although trucks appear to be larger every year, those surrounding our little Ford Courier as we fell into line at the customs area in Chetumal seemed gigantic. Our size must have made us conspicuous, for the chief customs officer, passing up several of those ahead of us, came directly to us. If we had any hope of his intending to move us to the head of the line, we were soon disillusioned.

Demanding to know what we were carrying in our well-locked vehicle, he asked for our keys and the list of contents. He opened the back door of the truck and peered into the neatly packed interior, studying our list as if mentally checking off each item. At first, he seemed satisfied. Then he began asking for clarification. Things like an old mimeograph machine and a typewriter were obvious. Boxes labeled dishes, silverware, cooking utensils, pots and pans, sheets, towels, curtains seemed obvious to us and had seemed so to those at Nazareth who had packed them. The customs officer wanted to know the exact number included in each package. We made some guesses, but guesses were not acceptable.

"We've got to unload this truck," he called to the drivers of the trucks lined up ahead of us and behind us, indicating his need of their assistance in that task.

Some of the men laughed; others voiced their impatience; all of them indicated their need to move on. The officer checked their credentials and approved their leaving Mexico, then went into his office, ignoring us completely. As soon as his door was closed his assistant approached us quietly and said, "Just be patient. He'll be out in a little while and let you through." Then he, too, disappeared.

Lynn laughed, then explained that when some of the customs officers think that they are dealing with "new" travelers, they try to extract *mordida*, a bribe, for letting them through in spite of something supposedly lacking in their report. Obviously this man realized that Lynn was not as new as he had hoped she was, for he soon came out of his office and waved us on. That hour's delay at the border served only as a reminder of how smooth and enjoyable our week's journey through Mexico had been.

Flags at doorways and posters on telephone poles were still declaring independence when the little Ford truck, tightly packed with household furnishings and office equipment, and bearing two SCNs, rolled down the Northern Highway from Chetumal, Mexico, to Belize City, Belize. The heavy jackets that had been a necessity ten days earlier had become extra baggage. Air conditioning would have been preferable, but it would be a long time before we would drive an air-conditioned vehicle again. Keeping cars and trucks in usable condition on Belizean roads in those days was all that could be expected. Anything extra just became something else to be jarred out of commission. Besides, there would be an occasional breeze from the Caribbean. No mechanical cooling device could match that.

A two-hour trip south on the Northern Highway brought us to Belize City where, at the intersection of Euphrates Avenue and Bosra Street, the heart of St. Ignatius parish is located. The church and the rectory face each other across Bosra at the corner. Bosra ends there, requiring the driver to turn right or left on Euphrates. The pedestrian may make one of those choices or continue directly across the street to the entrance of St. Ignatius School, which takes up a whole block and enrolls a thousand children.

Early afternoon classes were in session when we arrived, so all was quiet. We parked the truck at the curb in front of the rectory, went up the dozen or more steps to the front door where we were warmly welcomed by the pastor Bill Thro, SJ. Dick Perl, SJ, assistant, was out of town that day. After a brief visit, filled with accounts of the journey through Mexico and questions all around about plans for the immediate future, the parish team in formation escorted the faithful truck to its destination a block and a half away. We parked it beside a duplex, the first floor of which would be home and workshop for us for the next three years. With Bill's help, we began immediately to unpack, removing the things that we would need right away. After a few minutes, we recalled that we were supposed

Shortly after the SCNs' arrival, the photographer caught these fourth graders with Ransom (left) and Lynn (right) on Bosra Street. Behind them, and across Euphrates Avenue, is the main building of St. Ignatius School; other classroom buildings lie to the right and left. The porch of St. Ignatius Church on Bosra Street can be seen to the right, and the porch of the rectory to the left.

to have taken the truck to customs for approval before unpacking. I don't recall the outcome of our mistake. It may have cost us a fine. I tend to forget experiences of that nature. Whatever the outcome, we were home. Bill left us as we began setting up housekeeping. He invited us to supper in the rectory at five-thirty and told us that Mass at St. Ignatius would be at seven.

That evening's Mass is a sacred memory. It was there that we met many of the people who would become our very good friends and co-workers. As I recall that experience, it seems to me that those people were already in strong parish ministry, and we were indeed privileged to join them. Throughout the years that followed, Mass at seven every evening was the treasure-trove of the day. The grace of the Mass is priceless, of course. Following the Mass there would always be meetings of various groups for prayer and/or planning, classes in preparation for the sacraments, or simply friendly greetings, inquiry about the sick, accounts of happenings of one kind or another.

Lynn and I went home that evening, saying, "O God, it is good to be here." For us, life in Belize City had just begun.

Chapter Ten

CITY AS CENTER FOR SCN LAY MINISTRY EXPANSION

D ick Perl, SJ, recalls having transferred to St. Ignatius from St. Martin de Porres Parish in September 1981, just at the time when Belize became independent. He had thought that the SCNs were to come at the same time and that the team would set to work immediately to develop the Lay Ministry Program. His enthusiasm had not waned during the four months of waiting, so he was ready to begin now that the team was complete. He was soon to find out, however, that it would take many weeks of planning before the program could be launched.

Lynn's experience in the Stann Creek District from 1975 to 1981 had left her well prepared to initiate the Lay Ministry Program in the Belize District. The difference in geography, however, between the two districts, as well as the difference in concentration of population, would require considerable adaptation in planning. In contrast to Dangriga's population of 9,000 is Belize City's population of 70,000. Whereas Stann Creek District consists of Dangriga and more than a dozen villages, varying in population from several hundred in one to a thousand in another, Belize District consists of the City, a rural area, and two cayes—Caye Caulker and Ambergris Caye. Finally, although Lynn was acquainted with many of the people in the Belize District, it was necessary to spend some time meeting many more and in becoming better acquainted in order to work more effectively.

The picture of Swing Bridge (above) in the middle of Belize City serves as a good example of the difference between Stann Creek District and Belize District. The bridge is busy day and night. A sturdy wall in the middle separates pedestrians from vehicular traffic. The bridge is swung twice a day to let river traffic through. The main post office of the city occupies the first floor of the government building in the background.

At first glance, a review of the calendar of 110 West Street for the year 1982-83 suggests a routine parish schedule: Daily Mass at 7 p.m., three Masses on Sunday, two in the morning, one in the evening. It also lists the names of the Pastoral Team—two Jesuit priests, William Thro and Richard Perl (Bill and Dick) and two Sisters of Charity, Mary Lynn Fields and Mary Ransom Burke (Lynn and Ransom).

Taking time to read the notes on that calendar, however, reveals more than routine parish activity. The Pastoral Team, referred to hereafter as the Team, had had serious discussions from the beginning, resulting in Lynn's being asked to take full responsibility for the Ministers of the Word Program. It was understood that she would involve the full team according to the needs of the people and the talents and experience of the members of the Team. At the time recorded in the West Street calendar, one group of ministers was halfway through the preparation period and another was about to begin. Recorded for each month is a two-day period of intensive study of Scripture, Liturgy, Church Ministries, Group Dynamics, Public Speaking, Theology of the Sacraments, and Prayer.

Lynn and Dick were to work with the forty-eight teachers in St. Ignatius School, helping them to develop and maintain a Christian atmosphere. Lynn would go twice a month to Hattieville, a little village on the outskirts of the city assigned by the diocesan office to the care of St. Ignatius. She would observe the needs of the people, visit the sick, and take them Holy Communion.

Bill Thro and I would work on the Baptism Program, contacting parents and godparents, bringing them together for study of the rite and its meaning. When I took up that ministry, I was impressed by the seriousness of the godparents. Their sense of responsibility sometimes seemed to be greater than that of the parents. People, both children and adults, speak lovingly of godparents. At first I wondered to whom someone was referring by the name Goddy. I soon learned that it is a term of endearment for a godmother or godfather. Baptism was scheduled ordinarily for the first and third Sundays of each month; the number of candidates expected was eight to sixteen.

My chief assignment was Social Outreach. The record states that the title includes many topics but that we would approach them step by step. The first step was to conduct a much-needed parish census, beginning with the Yarborough area. The early record states: "There is Church property there. Someday, it is hoped, there will be a building on that property."

The census taking and the baptism program were closely associated. The latter was very time-consuming because baptisms were numerous and required visiting the parents and godparents as well as seeking out children who had "slipped through the cracks" and had not received the sacrament. I could have spent all my time on that program, for I was just finding my way around the city and trying to learn the "system" of house numbering, but it was not intended that I work with the baptism program full time. Therefore, when a fifth grade teacher became ill and an SOS signal went out for someone to direct her class for a play competition, I was free to volunteer. Recalling my years of experience in drama at various educational levels, I gladly accepted the challenge.

Well, experience in Louisville and Paducah, Kentucky, had not prepared me for coaching fifth-graders at St. Ignatius in Belize City! First, there was the language. The fifth graders spoke English but with an accent that was a combination of British and Creole. I needed an interpreter in order to understand them. How could I possibly direct them? Besides they had somehow conceived the idea that "to act is to proclaim at full volume." No amount of explanation could get them to speak otherwise.

I tried to withdraw, but did not succeed. Pleas came from all sides: "If you don't do it, the children can't be in the contest, and they have already learned their lines. They will be so disappointed."

Rather than disappoint the fifth graders, I agreed to go blindly on, and I was glad that I did. They didn't win a prize, but they evidently did very well, according to those who knew better than I the language and the style. The children were happy, and I learned the importance of approaching an unfamiliar culture gradually.

Belizeans speak English very well. There was a time, while Belize was a British colony, that Belize had the reputation of having the highest percentage of high quality English speakers compared with any other country in the world, except of course, Britain itself.

Learning to understand "Belizean" was a challenge that taught this listener really to listen. I recall steps in the process. For example, one day in a grocery store I listened to a little girl reading to the clerk the grocery list her mother had given her. There was hot *sauce*, string *beans,* white *bread,* sweet *potatoes*. Whereas we accent the adjective, Belizeans accent the noun. We are both consistent. We sing from *song* books, they from song *books*. We have *choir* practice. They have choir *practice*. Our trucks have *tail* gates, theirs, tail *gates*. I am sure there are exceptions, but listening to that little girl in the grocery store helped me to understand future conversations.

A brief recall of our early assignments in Belize City gives a bird's eye view of SCN entry there. To know something of the heart of that experience, however, it is necessary to enter more deeply into the lives of the people.

An event that made the beginning of that entry possible was the first weekend conference for people who hoped to become Ministers of the Word. It was held Saturday and Sunday, March 27-28, 1982, in the meeting room on the ground floor of St. Ignatius Rectory. The pastors and people throughout the Belize District had responded wholeheartedly with both encouragement and attendance. The latter, of course, had to be limited to those who might become part of the Lay Ministry Program. Well chosen as lead-speaker for that first conference in the Belize District was Charles Hunter, SJ. A native of Belize City, he will be remembered for his contribution to the very first session in Dangriga. His knowledge of the Scriptures and his ability to present them simply brought his message to the ministry candidates very effectively. His theme was "Call," stressing each person's call to ministry. Each presentation was followed by discussion, and the response was heartening.

Throughout the first day Charles Hunter had not been aware that his niece, Lupita Hunter, was one of nine persons who had died in a boat that had capsized Friday night. On Sunday he continued to talk about "Call," but now it became the call to life eternal. He offered the Mass of Resurrection for Lupita that afternoon at Holy Redeemer Cathedral. Attending, in addition to her family, were the faculty and students of St. Catherine Academy, where she had been a student, the Prime Minister and other government officials associated with Lupita's father, one of those officials. Needless to say, the candidates for Lay Ministry who had attended the weekend conference led by Charles Hunter, as well as many friends from nearby as well as from the States, were among the congregation that overflowed Holy Redeemer Cathedral that Sunday afternoon.

People unfamiliar with Mexico and Central America may not recognize the name Lupita as honoring Our Lady of Guadalupe, whose shrine is in Mexico City, and who is designated officially by the Church as Patroness of the Americas. Belizeans, on the other hand, are very devoted to Mary under that title. Many Belizeans bear the name Lupita.

That afternoon when I was with a group that had been rejoicing over the good things that were happening in the Church, someone remarked that frequently true joy is mixed with extreme sadness. We remembered, for example, Helen Trench, a teacher at St. Ignatius School, whom we had met at a tea on the lawn of the rectory two days earlier. We recalled how she had spoken so lovingly of her mother, who used to take her whole family to daily Mass, a practice that Helen had continued. The following morning Helen had suffered a heart attack and had died in an ambulance on the way to the hospital.

The purpose of the tea that Helen and many others had been attending was to raise seed money for the purchase of many things needed to initiate movement toward the St. Ignatius Fair, or the "Nashus" Fair, as it is more frequently called. That annual event is the one great means of support for the very large parish.

Ever since the summer of 1974, when Lynn and Susan had visited Belize in order to get acquainted with the country, the Sisters of Mercy had welcomed many an SCN at St. Catherine's. Major flights to Belize from the States land in Belize City, and it is frequently necessary to remain there some hours before going on to Dangriga or San Ignacio. Many SCNs have happy memories of those "stopovers," and the Community is truly grateful for the gracious hospitality of the "Mercies." In January 1982, however, when Lynn and Ransom took up residence in the City, a shift in custom occurred. Gradually, 110 West Street became the SCN "house of hospitality."

The first house guests were SCNs Julie Driscoll, Vocation Director, and Mary Elaine Zehnder, Director of the SCN Mission Office. They had seen Lynn and Ransom off from Louisville and then had taken a plane to Belize several days later, arriving, of course, before the two who had traveled by truck.

With our visitors using our place as the point of departure for the other missions, and with a number of commissioning ceremonies scheduled for the coming months, we, as well as our visitors, were traveling frequently. Commissionings occurred in Dangriga on January 30, in San Ignacio on February 7, in Punta Gorda on February 14. Each ceremony presented an opportunity, not only to recognize the new ministers and to encourage those who had been conducting the programs, but also to bring together the ten SCNs then ministering in Belize. After the San Ignacio meeting, Julie and Mary Elaine returned with us to Belize City. The evening of the following day, they joined us for a prayer session with eight young women who had shown an interest in learning more about our missions. Julie and Mary Elaine showed slides of SCNs in USA, India, Nepal, and Belize. The following day, we saw Julie and Mary Elaine off for the States.

Two weeks later, March 8, SCN Maria Vincent Brocato, Provincial of the Southern Province, arrived, and we left with her the following day for San Ignacio, where we joined all the other SCNs to discuss issues for the coming General Assembly of the Congregation.

After the meeting Maria Vincent stayed on to visit the Cayo and Stann Creek districts, as well as the Toledo District where Anna Marie Nalley, SCN, would soon be taking up residence.

Our team—Lynn and Ransom, Bill and Dick—continued to meet each week and to begin to take short monthly outings. The first trip was to Altun Ha, an ancient Maya ruin about thirty miles from Belize City. We took a picnic lunch and enjoyed exploring the ancient ruin. Although at that time excavation had not progressed to the extent reached at some of the other sites, Tom Barry calls it "one of the most impressive archeological sites in Belize" (*Inside Belize,* p. 80). He describes it briefly: "A major ceremonial and religious center, Altun Ha has two main plazas surrounded by a dozen structures, including the Temple of the Sun God, which rises sixty feet. A large water reservoir (inhabited by a nine foot crocodile), together with the ruin's proximity to the sea, help to explain its strategic location." One of the most interesting archeological finds in Belize is the famous Jade Head representing the Sun God, Kinich Ahau, found at Altun Ha. The original is carefully preserved in the capital at Belmopan. Many copies of it exist in both print and sculpture.

Besides planning for the ministry at hand, it was necessary to be associated with women and men religious of other congregations. In keeping with that responsibility, Lynn left Easter Sunday for Martinique to attend the meeting of the Major Superiors of the Antilles. Although geographically Belize is in Central America, in many ways it has more in common with the islands of the West Indies. It is not surprising, therefore, that the women and men religious in Belize were interested in meeting with the religious of those countries. Three years earlier the SCNs in Belize had elected Lynn to represent them for a period of three years.

During that first spring two SCN visitors came to share special programs. Margaret Dillier prepared more than a hundred people throughout the country to use the Laubach method of teaching reading. Miriam Corcoran, working chiefly with teachers at St. Ignatius School and mothers of children enrolled there, helped the teachers to see the value of drama in education. Miriam also made several trips to other parts of the country to share more widely that very effective method of teaching.

Throughout the summer, the back yard of 110 West Street was often the scene of liturgy followed by barbecue to celebrate the arrival, departure, and return of members of the several communities serving Belize. In addition to those already mentioned, there were SCNs Ann Kernen, en route to Dangriga, and Elaine Puthoff on her way to San Ignacio.

This residence later took on another role. In the fall of 1983, four SCN novices and their director Ann Whittaker made their home in Belize. Canonical novices Pat Caldwell and Irene Locario joined Ann in living at 110 West Street. Patsy O'Toole spent her second-year novitiate in Dangriga, and Mag Riggs spent hers in San Ignacio.

Two young women from Dangriga who had requested an opportunity to experience ministry in the City came for the week of August 1. With Ransom's assistance they studied the latest pastoral letter of the Caribbean bishops. The study of that letter prepared them to observe and learn from the visits they would make to the children's ward at the City Hospital; to the Office of the Council of Voluntary Services, directed by Ms. Auguet; and the Legal Aid Office under direction of Ms. Garbutt. They met Sadie Vernon, Director of the Belize Christian Council, a woman who has done more good than a thousand books could recount. Her office, with the assistance of volunteers, helps to meet needs of every kind, from those of young people on drugs to those of school children who have neither lunch nor money to buy it.

The visitors met Ms. Elaine Middleton at the Red Cross Society and Ms. Fox and Ms. Vernon at the YWCA. They visited several sick persons, including Mrs. Casassola, a woman in her nineties. A week was too short for in-depth experience. The two young women, however, did get an overall glimpse of social services in Belize City.

In addition to directing the novices, Ann Whittaker conducted religion classes in one of the schools. In this picture she is leading a class in the discussion of peace.

The summer activities closed August 30 with the annual candle-light procession in honor of Our Lady of Guadalupe. With partici-pation by all four parishes of the City, the large group assembled in the spacious playground of the Cathedral school moved throughout the city, praying and singing, and returned to the Cathedral for the closing ceremony. The purpose of the event was to pray for protec-tion from hurricanes to which Belize is extremely vulnerable.

Classes for preparing lay ministers continued throughout the fall and early winter months. Held once a month at St. Ignatius, the classes began at ten o'clock Saturday morning, continued until five in the afternoon, resumed at nine Sunday morning, closing in the afternoon with Mass at three. Friends and relatives housed those who came from the rural areas and the cayes. The midday meal was served at St. Ignatius both days.

On January 23, 1983, in Holy Redeemer Cathedral, Belize City, Bishop Robert L. Hodapp commissioned thirty-six women and men Ministers of the Word (lay ministers). That occasion, anticipated with so much joy, was tinged with sadness, however. Six weeks ear-lier, Blenda Heredia, one of the women who had been preparing for commissioning, died in an accident on the Northern Highway. She, her husband, her sister who was pregnant, and her sister's son were returning from Christmas shopping in Chetumal. It was after dark;

Mo Murray, SJ, and Michelle and Carlos Perdomo participate in a discussion at a lay ministry meeting at St. Ignatius in the early eighties.

there were no lights on the highway and none on grading equipment that had been left on the roadside. The car struck the equipment head on. The three passengers and the unborn child died. The driver, Blenda's husband, was seriously injured, but he survived. He was able to attend the commissioning, but he was too overcome with grief to approach the altar to accept the commission for Blenda. Their teenage daughter accepted it in his stead.

That sadness was intensified by information received that very morning about another accident that had occurred the day before. Victor Murno, a member of the next group of ministers, had been seriously injured. He would live only a few days. The recently commissioned ministers would be among the hundreds of people attending his funeral at St. Joseph's Church. Victor had been principal of a large high school. Someone remarked that everyone was at the funeral from the Prime Minister to the youngest freshman in the school. Once more we were made aware of the mingling of deep sorrow with heartfelt joy.

The commissioning ceremony at Holy Redeemer Cathedral was followed by dinner at St. Ignatius. As they celebrated, the new ministers talked about their assignments in their respective parishes within and outside the city. Part of their preparation had been to practice in the areas of those assignments. They talked also about classes for periodic review and refreshment, to which they were looking forward, and about plans that were in progress for a new group to begin in May—the group of which Victor Murno would have been a member.

A review of the names of the members of those groups on record at Nazareth, like other accounts in well-preserved annals, awakens valuable memories. Obviously, those lists are included because they are "firsts." No one pursuing information is likely to find many lists of that kind. Aware, however, of the value of history and of how important to history are the names of the people who participate in its development, I take an author's liberty of including below an account of the participants in the development of the Ministers of the

SCNs Mary Lynn Fields and Barbara Flores attend a meeting in Belize City in 1984.

Word Program in the Belize District. The lists at hand do not distinguish the commissioned ministers from their generous helpers in several very active parishes. Any lists reviewed at a distance and after lapse of time are bound to have errors and omissions. For any omissions or errors in the following list, I apologize.

Belize City

St. Ignatius
Sonia Ayuso, Florine Banner, Clarine Chimilio, Norma Garbutt, José Espat, Sr., Tomas Garcia, Olga Gentle, Mary Guzman, Marta Habet, Angelita Moody, Ivy Palacio, Sheila Rhodas, Juanita Saldivar, Sylvia Sampson, Marina Santos, William Scott

St. Joseph
Carmen Barnett, Horace Boyd, Rose Boyd, Lionel Kelly, Hortense Murray, Sarah Nicholas, Fernando Palacio, Sarita Palacio, Nicholas Pollard, Sr.; Louise Ramclam, Ernesto Reyes

Holy Redeemer
Alejandrina Burns, Alejandrina Gabourel, Jean Garel, Maurice Garel, Leo Garel, Alice Gegg, Edgar Gegg, Will Reynolds

St. Martin
Linda Arana, Isolene Enriquez, Hortense Haulze, Catherine Santos, Veronica Smith, Margaret Williams

Belize District

Caye Caulker
Ofelia Alamina, Gerald Badillo, Petrona Joseph, Claudia Reyes, Edwardo Reyes

Maskall
Martina Bardalez, Casilda Chan, Albina Ortega

Ladyville
Socarro Castillo, Joan Phillips, Concha Velasquez

San Pedro
Wilfredo Alamilla, Abel Guerrero, Lucio Guerrero, Martha Guerrero, Margaret Garcia

Burrell Boom
Dorothy Bradley, Heloise Meyers

Like the many stories recorded throughout this book, inspiring experiences abound among the ministers listed here. To tell them, however, would require another book. The Belize City parishes are similar to parishes in the States. Their very size, while increasing their capacity for good to be done, causes much of that good to be known by God alone, a situation quite acceptable to those who do it.

There can be no better way to recognize the need of more teachers in Belize than to visit a number of schools in action. This snapshot of some of the classes of St Ignatius School at early morning assembly offers an opportunity to glimpse the situation facing parishes and school boards. Although this is not a recent picture, the task has not diminished. Clement Wade, Superintendent of Schools, has said, "If you want to help, send us experienced teachers." There have been some questions about bringing in teachers when there are so many well prepared Belizean teachers. The answer is always, "Yes, we have many well prepared teachers, but not nearly a sufficient number to meet the need."

Chapter Eleven

HISTORY IN THE MAKING—
A PAPAL VISIT

In 1983 Pope John Paul II came to Central America to try to bring peace to the war-torn countries of that part of the world. Since Belize was the one peaceful country among them, there was some question as to whether he would visit there. The government of Belize prevailed upon him, however, to make one brief stop.

The Pope arrived at the Belize International Airport Wednesday, March 9, in time to celebrate Mass at 7:45 a.m. A large platform had been constructed on the tarmac, and the airport was closed for the duration of the unusual event. For the purpose of safety, people were admitted by tickets that had been carefully distributed. Present were Most Reverend Robert L. Hodapp, SJ, and Most Reverend Osmond P. Martin, Bishop and Auxiliary Bishop respectively of the Roman Catholic Diocese of Belize and Belmopan, together with priests, religious, and laity. Special places were reserved for official representatives of religious congregations as well as for representatives of other denominations. Sarah Ferriell officially represented the Sisters of Charity of Nazareth.

Special places were reserved for Dr. Minita Gordon, Governor General of Belize, and for Rt. Honorable George Cadle Price, Prime Minister, who was lector for the first reading of the Liturgy, Ephesians: 4.1-6, which contains those appropriate lines, "Make every effort to preserve the unity that has the spirit as its origin and peace as its binding force."

Five prominent Belizean men and women participated in offering intercessions. Representatives of eight ethnic groups—Creole, Chinese, Garifuna, Mestizo, Maya-Mopan and Ketchi, East Indian, and Lebanese—bearing gifts of Belizean products, formed the Offertory procession. Congregational singing included hymns familiar to Catholics generally, as well as the specifically Caribbean "Right Hand of God," and, finally, the National Anthem, "Land of the Free by the Carib Sea."

In the homily, His Holiness spoke of peace and of his journey through Central America in the hope of bringing peace. At the close of the Liturgy, he surprised everyone with a message especially for Belize. He said:

> I praise the divine providence that brought me to Belize!
> I give thanks to God for this opportunity to be in your midst
> today . . . and I am grateful to all of you, the people,
> for your manifestation of good will in my regard
> and for your wonderful welcome. God bless Belize.

Charles Hunter, SJ, in the *Jesuit Bulletin,* Summer, 1983, reviewed the visit of Pope John Paul, recording as well some of the comments on the visit appearing in the foreign press. He quoted especially the *Economist* of London, which wondered whether "the Pope's helpless plea to the bullets to stop whizzing about Central America, wasn't a mistake" (p. 12).

"Not so," said Father Hunter, noting the British publication's loss of its customary equanimity. Hunter then pointed out that, unlike their neighbors, the people of Belize are a "peaceful-minded people." He noted also that Prime Minister Price had spoken up for his people in reply to the *Economist.* Prime Minister Price wrote:

> Sir,
> Pope John Paul's Central American visit was not a mistake.
> Neither guns for civil war nor money for development
> did His Holiness bring. He brought the word of God to

comfort, to encourage and to dignify the people whose
cry he heard and answered because they count. Scripture
says man [sic] cannot live on bread alone, (but) . . . on every
word God utters (Matt. 4:4). The Central American and
Caribbean country of Belize thanks the Pope for his visit.

George Price
Prime Minister, Belize (p. 12)

Father Hunter commented, "The grateful letter was given first place
in the *Economist's* columns. The independent country of Belize is old
enough to speak for itself."

The *National Catholic Reporter,* March 18, 1983, describing the
event, quoted the pope as saying that while he "had come to visit the
Catholics" he came also "to proclaim to everyone the love of God . . .

*"I praise the divine
providence that
brought me to Belize.
I give thanks to God
for the opportunity
to be in your midst
today . . . and I am
grateful to all of you,
the people, for your
manifestation of
good will in my
regard and for your
wonderful welcome.
God bless Belize."*

the dignity of human persons." "His benediction—'God Bless Belize!'" the *Reporter* stated, "brought a vigorous ovation" (p. 27).

The *Reporter's* story also gave an account of attendance at the event by a number of people from Mexico. Quoting an unnamed priest, it stated, "At least four Mexican bishops, fifty or more priests and religious, and lots of Mexican buses [sic] came for the festivities." It was noted that visa and passport regulations were relaxed for the occasion. The only requirement was that the name be on a list submitted by the person's pastor.

The buoyant atmosphere generated by Pope John Paul's visit was pervasive. The period of the early eighties was a time of optimism in Belize. Although there was little change in the daily life of the people, the awareness of independence, a growing sense of ecumenism, and a developing appreciation of the place of the laity in the Church deepened.

Chapter Twelve

NEW HORIZONS: INCREASING NEEDS, DIMINISHING STAFF

I n 1984, the tenth year of the Lay Ministry Program in Belize, the parish teams realized that the lay ministers were becoming self-confident, in the best sense of that term. Those more recently commissioned needed some supervision, and all would need supplementary courses in preparation for recommissioning. Those just beginning would need the basic program, and the pastoral teams were always ready and eager to give the required courses. Throughout the program, however, the veteran lay ministers were becoming well qualified to assist with instruction and to supervise performance, a development that would free the pastoral teams to devote some of their time to other related work. Needs were so great and so numerous that the women religious were at a loss to know what they might offer to do, especially since they had to keep their basic commitment to lay ministry always in mind. Realizing their need of advice, those women—Dominicans, Sisters of Mercy, and SCNs all ministering in the city—came together one evening at St. Catherine Convent of the Sisters of Mercy to consider which of countless needs they might help to meet. They invited a friend, Eva Middleton, a Belizean woman in social service, to discuss the matter with them. Eva was delighted with the intent of the group. She hesitated not one moment to suggest that they assist young single mothers to find a way to assume responsibility for the support of their children.

She described the cycle in which many a young girl, eager to get out of an unsatisfactory situation at home and believing the promises a young man makes to her, joins him without any legal commitment. In many cases, he walks off and she is left with their child. Since she is not equipped to earn a living for herself and the child, she repeats her mistake, even though she may prefer not to do so, and the cycle continues.

Eva had visited a center in a neighboring country that she had been wishing might be duplicated in Belize. She hoped that our group might do something toward what she called a child development center. She suggested that as a first step we visit some of the homes that were, at that time, being used unofficially as day-care centers. Such a place was simply a house where one young woman was taking care of her child and the children of several other young mothers while those mothers went to work.

One visit was enough to convince us of the need to follow Eva's suggestion. There was no way that one young, inexperienced woman, despite her good intentions, could care for three or four or five little ones in a house that was not really equipped sufficiently to keep one child clean and properly fed. We were convinced that Eva was expressing a serious need, and we decided to do whatever we could to try to meet it.

We talked to Bishop Osmond P. Martin, who gave the effort his blessing and offered a lot near St. Martin de Porres Church, rectory, and school for the construction of a center. We wrote grant proposals and succeeded in getting enough money to start moving the project forward. We wrote also to our three communities, Mercies, Dominicans, and Charities, all of which contributed to the cause. Later, when the SCN Congregation received a gift for the missions, part of it was directed toward helping to support the Center. Interest from that gift continues to be received.

It would take four years to complete the plans, finance them, and build the Center. The lead article in the *Christian Herald* for January 1989 reads "Child Development Center Opens." The date of the opening was December 10, 1988. Bishop Martin blessed the

Center and, according to Belizean custom, declared it open. In his address he praised Phyllis Gaudreau, RSM, the director, and others who had worked to complete the Center.

The article called it "the brainchild of the Sisters of Mercy, Sisters of Charity of Nazareth, and the Dominican Sisters who work in Belize" (p. 1). The Bishop "cautioned of the need to maintain the Center well and called for the training of a Belizean to succeed Sister Phyllis as Director." The article also quotes Susan Lachapelle, RSM, stating that the goal of the Center is to assist women of the Martin de Porres area with their children while they work or develop skills needed in order to be employed. She explained further that children enrolled at the Center, infants through four years of age, are helped "to develop socially, psychologically, physically, and spiritually through a good education and nutrition program in an atmosphere of Christian love."

When, in 1997, I met the staff of the Center, teachers Gwen Cumberbach, Olilette Griffith, Therese Tench, and cook Leolin Humes, knowing that they had been with the Center from the beginning (1988), I was impressed with the solidity of the program and with the genuine loving care the children were receiving. The place was built to accommodate fifty children. It is always filled to capacity. It is reassuring also to know that a Belizean, Thomasa Smith, succeeded Sister Phyllis as Director and has held the position ever since.

Stories abound that reveal the good that has been accomplished. Three years ago vandals broke in, stole food, and damaged the building and some of the furnishings. The public response revealed the respect in which the Center is held. The group that initiated the movement had envisioned its becoming a first among several child development centers in Belize. The need continues, awaiting someone or some group to recognize it, to become inspired by the vision and, encouraged by the success of this one, to take the next step.

Establishing the Child Development Center took place between 1984 and 1988. During those years changes were occurring among

If the photographer had arrived earlier, the space would have been filled with little ones. The few in this picture will soon be picked up by mothers returning from the places where they have been employed. The staff remains until the last child leaves.

the team members at St. Ignatius. In 1984 Dick Perl moved to a mission in Honduras. In 1985 Elizabeth Miles, OP, joined Ransom at St. Ignatius, when Lynn went to study in Massachusetts. Bill Thro went to Dangriga and Father Ruoff to Belize City. Then, in 1986, when the Columban Fathers from Ireland accepted Bishop Martin's invitation to the Diocese, Father Sean McGrath succeeded Father Ruoff as pastor of St. Ignatius. During Bill Thro's last year at St. Ignatius, activities in the parish were carried on as usual. Elizabeth Miles took up direction of the lay ministers; Ransom assisted her. They both served in a variety of parish ministries.

Several times during the year 1985-86, the SCNs and OPs met to consider, as usual, "where we are and where we're going." One result of those meetings was the decision to hold a weeklong conference in order to have time to think through some of the questions that were frequently recurring. The conference, we agreed, should be held outside the usual workplace of any of the participants. We met in Guatemala City in September, a good time and a very good place, as our minutes demonstrate. In addition to carrying on very productive discussions, we had some refreshing experiences in the city and in the surrounding hills. We stayed one night in a small hillside hotel and assisted at Mass next morning in a little church nearby. It was really a storybook setting. There was no fiction about it, however. When we returned to our pews after receiving Holy Communion, our umbrellas were not in the benches where we had left them. The rain had stopped, however, so we were not really inconvenienced!

Down in the city they were celebrating annual Guatemalan Independence Day. When we looked for a restaurant for breakfast, the place most frequently recommended was . . .? You've guessed it, MacDonald's. So we went there. It resembled the Fourth of July in the States. The Guatemalan flag is blue and white, however. The absence of red with the white and blue assured us that we were not in the USA. Everything else was very much MacDonald's as we had known it, with copious decorations and favors galore for the children, and there were plenty of children to enjoy them.

The holiday spirit was contagious, but we resisted. Our party of eleven returned to the convent of the Sisters of the Ascension, where Dan Driscoll had arranged for us to stay and where we held our meetings. The Sisters there, whom Dan knew well, were most hospitable and very generous with space for the sessions we were planning to hold. Dan was, at that time, a member of Maryknoll, an experienced missionary, who, we were confident, would be an excellent facilitator with a fund of information.

Our Provincial, Emily Nabholz, SCN, had joined us for the conference. The others in attendance were the following: SCNs Sarah Ferriell, Adeline Fehribach, and Amina Bejos from Dangriga; Jane Karakunnel, Irene Locario, and John Loretto Mueller from San Antonio; Ann Kernen and Margaret Meisner from San Ignacio. Mary Ransom Burke, SCN, and Elizabeth Miles, OP, represented Belize City.

Provincial Emily Nabholz responds to questions about SCN ministry in Belize. On the right is Dan Driscoll, facilitator for the meeting.

The thoroughness of that three-day conference is reflected in a seven-page document entitled *Vision Statement, Goals and Objectives.* For those of us who participated in the conference, that statement acts as a catalyst, urging us to share a synopsis of it with those who have Belize's interest at heart today.

The first two pages lead to the statement of three goals: (1) to enable and empower lay leadership, (2) to reach out to abandoned areas in new ways, (3) to bond as SCN/OP faith communities in order to nourish spirit-filled ministry.

Standing alone, those goals may appear to be merely statements of wishful thinking. They are, however, preceded by an account of discussions that review the founding of the program more than ten years earlier. That review includes genuine appreciation of those who had done the ground work, honest evaluation of development since that time, and expressions of concern regarding areas where there is experience of incompleteness, confusion, and frustration. Those comments conclude with a declaration:

> Yet, our deep desire for collaboration and mutuality, our long-ing to help in the development of confident Belizean lead-ership, our earnestness to promote the value and dignity of women, our experience of the oppression of women in a Church that we love, our concern for the poor and aban-doned—these areas of ministry move us to be unsatisfied with the present reality. Our pledge of loyalty to all we value and cherish binds us to speak the truth as we see it, in love.

The Vision Statement acknowledges "the deep faith that we experience in the people of Belize and in their ability to maintain that faith." That faith-filled response to the "reality of life," the statement continues, "is a support and challenge to our own faith journey." Then the authors of the statement acknowledge themselves to be learners, "willing to be transformed through ministry with the laity and with the ordained ministers."

The authors agreed, in general, on how the goals were to be achieved. They set up a schedule for reporting on this conference to Bishop Martin, to authority in the communities involved, and to respective pastoral teams. A date was set by which responses to those reports were to be reviewed. Finally, each team met separately to determine how to implement the goals applicable to the particular locality.

Liz and Ransom returned to Belize City, refreshed and enthusiastic, to begin implementation in the Belize District. Liz shared with the lay ministers the results of the planning at the conference, began the development of a parish council, and worked toward inclusion of lay membership on the parish team. Ransom resumed her work with the program of instruction for the Sacrament of Baptism, inviting lay ministers to work with her, both in instruction proper, and in the revision of the instruction booklet. In the parish Liz continued as advisor for the Legion of Mary and Ransom for the Sodality. Liz expanded the recently initiated religious education program at Hattieville on the outskirts of the city. (Hattieville is so named because it is the place to which refugees from the city were taken when Hurricane Hattie struck in 1961. The refugees stayed, and the refuge became a village.)

Ransom continued to develop the religious education program in Port Loyola, an extension of the city, originally the site of St. John's College and named for St. Ignatius Loyola, founder of the Jesuits who administer the college. The school had been moved inland after two hurricanes took many lives and demolished several buildings.

Liz enabled lay ministers to serve weekly at Maskall and Caye Caulker. Ransom worked toward the development of the St. Vincent de Paul Society. Women of the parish had, for a long time, been doing St. Vincent de Paul ministry, and some of the men, especially Leo Garel, had tried to establish a center for collecting clothing and other things needed by the poor. It was evident that, with an organized plan, those zealous, caring people could reach a greater number of needy people. A workshop was held September 27, 1986, when a regional officer came to Belize to establish the Society officially. Representatives from most parishes in Belize attended the program.

It was one of those "ideas whose time had come." Many parishes saw the need of the Society and the value of becoming a part of it. The year 2000 found a number of very active conferences (units) throughout the country. Many people entered into the work. Recently I had an opportunity to visit with some of the members of the Society. Sonia Ayuso, Florine Banner, Marta Habet, Marina Santos, and Amelia Scott had been among the first to respond in St. Ignatius Parish in the 1980s. They and many others continue to carry on the ministry that has grown and diversified.

Liz and Ransom attended meetings of the organization *Violence against Women* and lent support to the organization generally. They continued to work with other women religious in the city on such programs as the *Child Development Center*. They kept always in mind the decisions made at the Guatemala meeting and used every opportunity to effect their implementation. They continued also to be very busy with projects in which they were already involved. For example, Liz had developed a program in which she had enlisted lay ministers to accompany her on regular visits to women in the local jail.

Then, just as there had been a need for a pre-school in the heart of Belize City, so, according to mothers in the outskirts of the city, there was need for a primary school in the section called Yarborough. An appeal from those mothers was heard during a census-taking project that we conducted for St. Ignatius Parish with the assistance of students from Boston College, known as Jesuit International Volunteers or JIVs. This on-going volunteer program conducted by the universities administered by the Jesuits gives the volunteers priceless experience and the people they serve inestimable assistance. In the beginning of the Yarborough program the purpose was to conduct a good parish census while there were volunteers at hand. Once that program was under way, however, mothers of children of primary school age began approaching us saying,

"The older children can walk from here to 'Nashus'," as St. Ignatius is fondly called, "but the little ones cannot. 'Nashus' is crowded anyway. Can't you do something to get classes for Infant One and Two closer to our homes?" I agreed to try. Thus began the tale of how a whole parish developed out of the urgent plea of a group of mothers for the opening of an infant school.

Rick, Steve, and Dave, JIVs (Jesuit International Volunteers), with young men at the Youth Hostel in Belize City near St. Ignatius School.

Chapter Thirteen

EDUCATION:
A TOP PRIORITY

The number of children accounted for by the mothers who had expressed the need, as well as results of the census in general, showed that a building would have to be constructed to house a new Infant School in the Yarborough area. Tacit understanding remained that after Infant Two, the children would walk the many blocks to "Nashus" as their older brothers and sisters had been doing. A question must have been in most minds, however: "How will 'Nashus' accommodate that many new Standard One students every year in addition to those completing the 'Nashus' Infant Two?" Belize City was growing, especially in the Yarborough area. The number of buses serving the area was increasing, some of them phonetically labeled "Yarbra."

In order to preserve the momentum just begun, I went to Bishop Martin with the question, "It is evident that classrooms are needed; where do you suggest that the building be constructed?" Bishop Martin responded with assurance, "The diocese has always done long-range planning. There is land in Yarborough that belongs to the Church. It is on Fabers Road, next to Excelsior High School where you and the ladies from St. Ignatius have been holding Sunday-School classes."

A group that attended Mass offered by one of the priests from St. Ignatius Parish one Sunday afternoon a month at Excelsior High School on Fabers Road (with permission from John Young, principal of that school) stand before a sign that reads: "Future Port Loyola Catholic Church Site."

Four years later, this building stood on the spot where those parishioners had stood. It housed the Infant School and a chapel. Now, the school consists of several large buildings, and beside it stands a parish church—St. John Vianney

That was familiar territory. Not only had we been holding catechism classes there, but, as Doris Brooks, long-time resident of the area, recalls, a group from St. Ignatius had asked that one of the priests offer Mass there one Sunday afternoon a month. Their purpose was to help people in the area who were unable to walk to St. Ignatius and who did not have transportation.

John Young, Principal of Excelsior High School, had given permission for the use of some classrooms. "The week before each third Sunday," Doris reminded me, "our St. Ignatius group would distribute throughout the neighborhood flyers announcing the Mass. Bill Thro or Dick Perl would offer the Mass; the St. Ignatius group would lead the singing with guitar accompaniment."

Responding enthusiastically, then, about the site, yet hesitating to leave the next step to the very busy bishop when months can slip away so rapidly, I remarked, "I suppose we'll need the deed to the land if we are going to build on it. You have the deed, Bishop?"

"No, the deed is in the Lands Department in the government building down the street. If you go over there, just tell them I asked you to pick it up."

With that began a search for the deed that was eventually found in the presbytery. A wise bishop many years ago had foreseen the expansion of Belize out Yarborough way and had secured the land for that expansion. A careful secretary, who had become familiar with the documents on file, produced the deed as soon as she became aware that it was needed. That, however, was only one step in the process. Even a two-room school building requires cleared land, architectural plans, a building permit, and builders to carry out the plans. The land was easily identified as described in the deed. That it was not in condition for immediate use was evident, however. It was overgrown with mangrove trees and vines and weeds and tropical wildflowers.

At first there was no visible movement to clear the land in preparation for the building of a school. In order, therefore, to keep the project alive a number of people of Yarborough, many of them parents of children who would eventually attend the school, and others like me, went out one Saturday afternoon with machetes and hacked away at growth of years. We made little progress, but the attempt did get publicity. The Bishop called in the leader of the "publicity stunt" and gave her strict orders to "not cut down any more trees." She agreed but asked, "Is there some company we could employ to clear the land?"

"A company to clear the land in Belize?" responded Bishop Martin with a hearty laugh. "In Belize we clear our own land," he said.

"Well, Bishop, you tell us not to cut down trees. We need a school. We have the land. There is a group ready to raise funds. How do we clear the land?"

Bishop Martin became very serious. "Sister," he said, "call Mayor Lizama. Tell him about the situation. Ask him to send some of the occupants of the jail. They'll clear the land in a few hours. But, also talk to the ladies who see the need of the school, and ask them to have a good dinner prepared for the men."

Having been reared in a land that would not have approved of "using" prisoners in that way, I questioned it. Both the Bishop and the Mayor assured me that the prisoners would welcome the change of venue and the good food. The reality proved them right. Mayor Lizama approached the area representative, the Honorable Henry Young, who saw to it that, with all proper government approval, the prisoners came to clear the land. Doris Brooks generously invited the ladies to use her kitchen to prepare the food. Mrs. Nessie Young furnished transportation, as Doris and other zealous promoters of the cause went about soliciting food or donations for the feast.

After the land was cleared, it was necessary to procure and deposit landfill, because Belize City is below sea level. That done, a vigorous campaign for funds began. The need for the school had become so evident that people at all levels took an interest. First the people of St. Ignatius Parish, then the business community, encouraged by the Hon. Henry Young, lent support. Bishop Martin and the Catholic Diocese supplied all that was needed to begin constructing what would become the center building of a complex that would grow year by year, eventually accommodating 650 students and a parish church. The dedication ceremony took place the evening of March 25, 1988, just five years after that group of strong, caring, sensitive mothers expressed the urgency for carrying into fruition a plan begun by a farsighted bishop, who had secured the land at least twenty years earlier, and completed by hundreds of people, including the volunteers from Boston College who lent enthusiastic support for a greatly needed parish church and school.

By the time of the dedication I was teaching at Divine Word College in Iowa, but an invitation to the ceremony and a newspaper clipping describing it are among my prized possessions. When I visited Belize nearly ten years later, Ms. Annie Wade, principal since opening day, conducted me on a tour of the entire compound. What a joy it was to see so great a need being so well met.

It was certainly appropriate that the new parish, St. John Vianney, with its large school, should develop next to Excelsior High School. As different as the two schools are, they are both dedicated to learning—to learning as needed at a particular place, for particular people, at a particular time.

Jesuit Brother Karl Swift, a Belizean, had been teaching at Excelsior for more than twenty years, when the new school was becoming its neighbor. He knew the history of Excelsior and was glad to share it. According to Karl, it opened as Curtis Junior High School about 1971, then became Excelsior in 1977. It began, he says, as a school for students who were unable to pass the tests for the regular high schools. The more than 200 students were poor. One wonders how many of them were able to pay the tuition, $10.00 a month. The school was similar to Excelsior in Jamaica, a school that was ridiculed at first but that went on to become the largest school in that country. Excelsior took students where they were in the learning process, encouraged them, helped them to develop. "It moved to the present site in 1981," said Brother Karl, "with about 150 students. During the period 1988 to 1992 the enrollment was about 500. Now there are 390 students."

"In 1993 free tuition was offered in all schools," Brother Karl said, "and some Excelsior students went elsewhere." He has seen a number of Excelsior graduates acquire really prestigious positions. "Six grads," he said, "are on the present faculty. One of those teachers will soon have her Master's Degree. One is a librarian, one a secretary, one teaches physical education. And we have graduates in government in this and in other countries." Brother Karl has taken great joy in seeing the success of those and of many other graduates of Excelsior. He has high praise for Alexander Lamb, founder of the school, a Belizean who now lives in Chicago.

Development in education in Belize during the previous twenty years had been built upon a firm foundation. Franciscan and Dominican missionaries have, at various times since the mid seventeenth century, tried to meet the needs of the various settlers. When the Jesuits responded to the call to Belize in the mid nineteenth century, their first efforts were to take the Church to the many settlements of the country, some of which could be reached only by boat.

By 1887 it was possible to establish a school for young men at the presbytery. By 1896 that school was moved into a separate building (Richard Buhler, *A History of the Catholic Church in Belize*, p. 66). In December 1879, two Jesuits had visited the provincial house of the Sisters of Mercy in New Orleans, asking for sisters to teach in Belize City. Negotiations of four years finally resulted in five Sisters of Mercy going to Belize in 1883. They taught in Holy Redeemer School, the parish school of Holy Redeemer Cathedral, and at St. Catherine Academy. The very fine annals of the Sisters of Mercy, excerpted by Yvonne Hunter, RSM, in her monograph *The Sisters of Mercy in Belize—1883-1983* present a detailed account of those early years.

That account reveals the many difficulties that had to be overcome to assure soundness and continuity. In the beginning the relationship of the Belize community to the provincial house in New Orleans was not clear. That lack of clarity led to a temporary separation. The heavy pressure of World War I took its toll on everyone in the small country of Belize. There was unexpected illness and there were many deaths among the members of the Sisters of Mercy.

Among those early Sisters of Mercy, according to their annals, was one Kentuckian, Evelyn Stahr. A certified teacher, she had been teaching in western Kentucky several years when she saw in the *Sacred Heart Messenger* an advertisement for St. Catherine Academy in British Honduras, as Belize was then called. That advertisement was not simply to attract students but also to invite young women to become Sisters of Mercy and missionaries to British Honduras.

Through that advertisement, God called Evelyn Stahr to Belize, where she became Sister Mary Berchmans, RSM. She taught at Holy Redeemer Boys' School from 1916 to 1932, when she became principal, 1932 to 1938. Sister taught at St. Catherine Elementary School and at St. Catherine Academy after 1938. She died in 1976 at the age of eighty-eight and is buried in Belize.

That account of Sister Mary Berchmans's life in Belize, like many another synopsis, tells only part of the story. The circumstances of Evelyn Stahr's entrance into the Sisters of Mercy were unusual, to say the least. Attracted by what might seem to be a mere glance at an ad in a magazine, she pursued with little hesitation all that the ad offered. Then, according to the annals, she met an unpredictable obstacle when she reached Belize, as the following excerpt shows:

> August 2, 1914: Our postulant, Miss Stahr, arrived on the steamer and had to go to Quarantine for a few days.
> August 3, 1914: Reverend Mother and Sister Mary Mercedes went to Quarantine Station to see Miss Stahr.
> August 6, 1914: Sisters Mary Louise and Teresa went in a carriage to Quarantine Station to bring Miss Stahr home. On her arrival Rev. Mother gave her the cap. She had to go to Quarantine for five days. (p. 58)

As Yvonne Hunter further explains, "because yellow fever was raging again in New Orleans, passengers embarking from that port were detained in quarantine upon arrival for a few days before being allowed to join family or friends." Hunter further points out that Sister Mary

Berchmans "did the archives at St. Catherine Convent which she kept meticulously until a few months before her death." Hunter adds that "during her retirement Sister received many visits from her 'old boys.'" Indeed, referring to Holy Redeemer Boys' School, Yvonne states that Sister Mary Berchmans "was quite a legend there" (p. 58).

Besides being a Kentuckian, Sister Mary Berchmans was related to three Sisters of Charity of Nazareth, Rachel and Clara Willett and Mary Wedding. Their grandfather and Sister Mary Berchmans's father were brothers. Several years ago Rachel followed up the family story of "Cousin Birdie." She traveled to Belize, talked with Sisters of Mercy, who had fond memories of Sister Mary Berchmans, and visited Sister's grave. Rachel says:

> As I met the Mercy Sisters at St. Catherine Academy, one after another said, "Sister Mary Berchmans taught me history." When I visited SCNAs Simeon and Juanita Joseph and was asked what brought me to Belize, I told them that I wanted to see the place where years ago I had addressed letters for grandmother to Sister Mary Berchmans. At the mention of that name, Juanita exclaimed, "Sister Mary Berchmans! She taught me history. She was my senior homeroom teacher! Every year she would print on her board *Not every beautiful girl is good, but every good girl is beautiful.* We loved her. She was a great teacher."

"That visit," says Rachel, "brought to a close the childhood experience." She recalls writing on a long envelope the long name Sister Mary Berchmans Stahr, when, as a child of ten, she "visited grandma and grandpa in the big red brick house at the top of the hill in Fancy Farm, Kentucky." Whereas Rachel's visit to Belize completed for her an experience begun in childhood, her account of it here emphasizes the place of education in both Kentucky and Belize in the early twentieth century.

That education continued to hold high priority throughout the twentieth century in Belize is evidenced by the history of Delille Academy in Dangriga. The Holy Family Sisters from New Orleans have been teaching there in elementary school and high school since 1898. In the late eighties Sister Judith Therese Barial, a member of that community, and a faculty member of Ecumenical College (high school), found herself spending more time assisting and coaching outside the classroom than in holding her regular classes.

Taking each young woman who came to her for assistance at whatever might be the point of need, Judith gradually initiated classes in English language, mathematics, Spanish, Belizean history, music, sewing, and Christian Living. Beginning with sessions on Saturday and during vacation time, Judith soon requested and received permission to withdraw from her regular teaching assignment at Ecumenical and to hold classes full time in what became known as the Christian Youth Enrichment (CYE) program, accommodated on the ground floor of the convent.

The students who came asking for help were from varied backgrounds and had differing abilities. Some were dropouts for whatever reason; some did not have all the requirements for entry into high school. All were finding themselves in need of more education than they had been able to acquire. They and others who followed them were fortunate that Judith was able and willing to try to meet their needs. I watched that little school coming into existence in 1989 with the help of grants and donations.

Eleven years later, according to the program distributed at graduation, the student body numbered 150 and the full-time faculty 10 certified teachers. The school was accredited in 1996 by the Ministry of Education. In the same year the name was changed to Delille Junior Academy, honoring the founder of the Holy Family Sisters. In 1998 it became a full four-year academy.

In the souvenir program, at graduation, *Horizon 2000*, Bishop Martin wrote:

> Delille Academy is a special education institution that stands as a witness to justice, peace, and compassion. It represents the spirit of Mother Henriette Delille and the true charism of the Holy Family Sisters. The final year of the 20th century (1999)

has been a year of increased challenges to this young institution.
. . . However the Honorable Sylvia Flores, speaker of the House
and a true friend of the Holy Family Sisters, did much to solicit
the aid of the Government and US Embassy to help overcome
some of these challenges. As we pray miracles to happen
through the intercession of Henriette Delille, I deeply believe
that we are going to see positive responses and welcomed solu-
tions to the challenges that face this infant institution.

From the early twentieth century, then, into the beginning of the
twenty-first, education, both traditional and innovative, continues to
hold high priority in Belize. The next chapter picks up that "thread
that runs so true," and follows it into a time of transition.

*Bishop Martin encourages
young people in both
formal and informal
situations. Here he chats
with little ones in Jalacte.
Note that he wears the
usual dignified business
suit called the guayabera.
To see the bishop in
formal liturgical vestments,
see Chapter Eighteen.*

Chapter Fourteen

THE NINETIES:
A TIME OF TRANSITION

Whether the focus of history be on nations or local areas, within specific timeframes or on the flow of life in general, the people involved must live and act at particular times in particular places. Highlights in the previous chapter spanned more than a century. The period of the present focus is the 1990s in Belize City and villages immediately surrounding it.

In the late eighties Bishop Martin succeeded in bringing Columban Fathers from Ireland to serve in some of the parishes in Belize. That was the time when the Church everywhere was beginning to experience diminishment in the number of men and women serving in church-related ministries. The Columbans made a genuine contribution. They served well in Sacred Heart Parish in Dangriga and in some of the rural parishes near Belize City. Sean McGrath renovated and greatly enhanced the physical plant at St. Ignatius in the City. Flannan O'Keeffe was instrumental in getting the new Belize City Parish of St. John Vianney off to a good start. Their manner was different, however, from that of the pastors who had encouraged lay ministry. They were courteous and kind, but they had their own style of ministering—a style that did not encourage ministry by the laity. Their tenure was short, only ten years. Like other religious congregations, the Columbans were experiencing diminishment in numbers. When, as a result, they had to withdraw from some of their missions, they withdrew first from those most recently entered.

Other departures in the 1980s included those of women religious. In 1988, Elizabeth Miles, OP, was elected President of her congregation, a position requiring her to return to Kentucky. Ransom had returned to Kentucky the previous year. Neither was replaced.

Barbara Flores and Irene Locario, both Belizean SCNs, remained at the SCN house in the city, Barbara as Diocesan Director of Religious Education for the Catholic Schools, and Irene as teacher in St. Martin de Porres School. Soon they were joined by SCNs Jean Kulangara, who came from India, and Ann Kernen, and by Eileen Hannon, OP. Jean was Local Manager of Schools and Associate Pastoral Administrator of St. Martin's Parish. Eileen was Director of the Lay Ministry Program in the Belize District. Ann served as assistant to Eileen and as part-time Vocation Director. Part of the time Claire McGowan, OP, psychologist, was a member of the local community while offering pastoral support services in Belize, Guatemala, and Nicaragua. Completing the community were Mary Hartnett, RSM, Director of the Mercy Clinic, and Cecilia Crittenden, Dominican Sister of the Sick Poor.

Barbara Flores, SCN, then Director of Religious Education for the Diocese, conducted retreats and in-service education programs for teachers at Trinidad Farm, a retreat center near Belize City.

In August 1988 Elaine McCarron, SCN, came from Washington D.C. to assist Barbara and Jean with their part in the National Catholic Teachers Convention, giving workshops in fourteen schools and working with catechists in the villages. Their place of residence, known as Casa de Paz, had many visitors. The guest book at open house in November registered a hundred signatures. The remainder of the school year, through the month of July, was one of many "comings and goings," according to the annals of Casa de Paz. At the end of that year Cecilia returned to the United States, "having completed her two-year contract in Belize." Sister Jean "was leaving Belize City for the Toledo District."

After that the full house at Casa de Paz continued to diminish. The occupants were gradually called elsewhere one by one. Two have been accounted for. Ill health soon caused two more to leave: Mary Hartnett, RSM, returned home to her community's house in Connecticut, and Eileen Hannon, OP, to hers in Massachusetts. Mary's health improved; Eileen died within a year. Her death surprised and saddened everyone whom she had embraced in her recent very active leadership in the lay ministry program. Mid-decade, Barbara began the pursuit of further education at Northwestern University in Chicago. Irene continued her ministry of teaching, but moved into secondary education at St. Catherine Academy. Claire was elected to her community's governing board in Kentucky. Ann returned to Kentucky, to a mission in Appalachia, and later to administration in her community's Southern Region.

During the General Assembly at Nazareth in 1990, there was a called meeting of SCNs and Dominicans who were especially interested in the Belize Mission. Susan Gatz, Southern Regional, chaired the meeting. Sisters who had had recent experience in Belize reported on the then current state of the mission. In summary, they said that Belize needs our continued presence, especially in the villages; that we need more SCNs, OPs, and SCNAs to be in mission there, both full time and part time; and that there are many ways in which "folks at home can assist." It was suggested that the Mission

Office at Nazareth, through *SCN Mission News*, increase awareness of Belize and its needs.

On file in the Mission Office is a paper signed by most of the people present at that meeting, stating things that they were offering to do in response to requests made there at that time. I hold that paper with reverence. There are forty-nine names on it, all of whom promised to pray. Surely those prayers have served to sustain our Belize mission and all who have ministered there.

In addition to prayer, the list includes a great variety of "things I could do": offers to give workshops in counseling, skills development, and teacher education; courses in theology, liturgy, and health care; offers to make the mission and the need known among people who are in a position to help professionally or financially. Several people offered books or other kinds of publications; others offered to write congresspersons who might help politically. One person made a commitment "to continue raising $50.00 a year for the cause."

All of those offers were accepted gratefully. Those that could be were put into effect immediately. Regretfully, at that time, we had neither the personnel nor the finances nor facilities for utilizing them all. As we review them now in the light of recent developments, we hope that more of them may be revived.

After that meeting, referred to as the Belize Party, the SCN Mission Office began immediately to report on it, to try to implement some of the many suggestions and offerings that resulted from it, and to try to relate the outcome to the people in Belize. Barbara Flores and Mary Ransom agreed to co-chair a movement called the "Belize Connection," Barbara working in Belize and Mary Ransom at Nazareth, using the Mission Office as the link, and the publication *SCN Mission News* as a means of publicizing it.

After they had worked separately for a year, Ransom went to Belize in October 1991, to work directly with Barbara for several weeks and to interview at least twenty-five people, asking them to critique the plans and to make suggestions. Actually they interviewed twenty-four people plus a group of twenty-five lay ministers and a group of about fifteen village people.

> We prepared our tentative plan in proposal form as follows:
>> To explore the possibility of establishing several centers out of which persons may go into villages to be present to the people there and to serve them according to their needs.
>
> For rationale, we stated:
>> Belize is a country of 8,600 square miles of mainland and 266 square miles of off shore islands. The 300,000 Belizeans live in two cities, seven towns, and 160 villages and settlements.
>>
>> Over the years some experienced missionaries have said, "if a group could be located in a center, out of which individuals or small groups might go regularly to the villages in that area, staying as long a time as proves helpful, the people might be better served."

Ninety percent of the people interviewed agreed that that statement is true. Included in the interviews were questions about greatest needs. We noted those special **needs** and then summarized them as follows:

Expression of Needs

   I. Religious Education, Spirituality, Prayer;

  II. Ecumenism: religious unity, a healing of the disruption caused by "new" churches;

 III. Health Care: education in hygiene and methods of preventing disease; nutrition education; care of sick and elderly;

 IV. Child Care;

  V. Education: literacy, teacher education, emphasis on preschool, high school, art, music, crafts, pottery; construction; tutoring;

 VI. Empowerment: building of self-confidence; development of leadership ability, among women especially; development of social skills and capacity for adult commitment;

VII. Marketing of produce and crafts;
VIII. Organization: management, team-building, communication, coordination, direction, planning;
  IX. Global Awareness and Justice Issues;
  X. Control of drugs and alcohol.

Encouraged by the acceptance and enthusiasm of those whom we interviewed, we took our proposal immediately to Bishop Martin, who accepted and blessed the plan. Even before talking with the Bishop, we realized that we would have to begin with one center. When we talked with him, he explained the necessity of moving slowly even with that one. Chapter Seventeen traces the development of that Center in Independence and of the villages served from there.

Before we had made a decision about where to establish the first center, we considered several possibilities recommended by Bishop Martin. One of the most appealing of those was called Belize Rural. The greatest appeal was in the area itself and in its needs. Added to that was the realization that to serve Belize Rural the Center would necessarily be in Belize City, making it easier than having to set up a center in a new location.

To know Belize City without knowing Belize Rural is to have only a partial knowledge of the Belize District. We found that out while searching for the right center. One Sunday in October 1991, with Vickie and Pat Conroy, volunteers from Canada, I visited three of the ten villages in that District: Bermudian Landing, St. Paul's Bank, and Rancho Dolores. It was Rancho that charmed me, not the place so much as the people who lived there.

In a little grocery store, we found Jane and Faustino Perez. Although she is elderly and blind, Jane manages the store. A price list hangs on the wall at left. People come in, tell her what they want; she tells them to take it off the shelf. She adds the items "in her head" and asks the shopper to leave the payment on the counter. Miss Jane is so well loved that no one takes advantage of her. Faustino is a farmer, quieter than Jane, but very loving and supportive of her.

That Sunday morning, Jane reflected on the days before her blindness. She loved to sew and to weave and to make doilies. She often won first prize for her orange and guava jellies. Jane is still very much in demand as a storyteller. When we visited her, she had recently won first prize, $225.00, in a storytelling contest in Belize City for her story about a rhinoceros. Learning her own life story was like reading a chapter of a book. It was easy to see that Jane had been a leader, a gifted woman who had used her gifts well for others—her husband and children as well as her neighbors. For a long time the village had looked to her for leadership. Since her activities had become limited, it was evident that the village was slowing down.

Jane had hoped that others, who she was certain could do it, would take the leadership role and get the little village to pull together. The problem, as she saw it, was the pulling apart of a once strong Catholic community.

Jane recalled the days when a priest would come down on Saturday by boat from Belize City, visit the people, hear confessions, stay all night, and offer Mass on Sunday morning. Now that there are so few priests, she said, Father comes only once a month on Sunday, offers Mass, and has to leave soon afterwards.

Ministers of other denominations come in more often, hold services, and mingle with the people. The people, she said, following the strong urge within them to worship God, respond to the cordiality, the sociability, the music, the prayer. The Catholics who attend those services, she said, still call themselves Catholic.

Jane regrets the present situation, but she said, "God is all. God will take care of us. I'll never change my church. The only thing I change is my clothes."

Listening to Jane as she recalled graphically her sixty-seven years in that little village was like watching a film with Jane as the heroine (my casting, not hers). She said,

> From time I got sense (eight years old), this was all bush. Fader used to come from Belize City by boat and stay two or three days. An Anglican teacher came from June to December.

Teacher followed teacher, even one in arts and crafts now and then. I go until I grown, but there were no exams and no way to go to high school.

We had to go to Belize City in a dory. No roads. We'd leave at midnight on Sunday, sleep in the dory, arrive in the City about three a.m. At daylight we'd have a meal. Get home Wednesday or Thursday.

When I was eleven, I began helping my daddy with the dory. Once a boat passed, splashing so much water, dory turned over, but we managed to save ourselves.

We had to take sick people to Belize City. Took two of my sisters. One died, buried in Belize City. Pa died when I was nineteen. I worked out to help my mother, did housework for $1.00 a week.

I helped my mother. Then (the 1930s) eggs were three for five cents, meat ten cents a pound, rice ten cents a hand.

Married this man six years later, had seven sons, two daughters. Saw them all through college. They want us to live with them, but the country is sweet. My husband cook. My son cook.

We asked about the village of Rancho Dolores, and she gave us a detailed account of the approximately twenty-five families that form the population of about 300 people. When we reluctantly rose to leave, we were urged to wait while Faustino fetched a pumpkin to take with us.

Our next stop was St. Paul's Bank, somewhat smaller. There we visited Mary McFadzean, who was looking forward to the celebration of her ninety-fifth birthday. She had had twelve children, she told us, of whom six were still living, two girls, four boys. The youngest, she said, was fifty-nine. Many family members, old and young, were coming and going. We were invited to stay, but had to decline in order to move on to our next stop. We promised them and ourselves that we'd come back for a real visit.

We had looked forward to Bermudian Landing, for we had been told that we would meet a group of children there. The group was smaller than we had anticipated and not very eager to talk. There were no adults with them, only two older girls, students at Pallotti High School in Belize City. Vickie and Pat tried leading the children in some games. They participated, but not enthusiastically. We decided that they must have had something planned and that our visit was interfering with those plans, so Pat gave them some little souvenirs and we went on our way.

It was through Josella Flowers, SAC, who ministered with Columban Father Seamus O'Neil, that I had met Vickie and Pat. Josella had, for some time, been visiting villages in the "District." When I asked her to suggest three villages to visit that would serve as a sample of that district, she responded immediately with the three to which I have just referred.

During our conversation she mentioned eight others: Lamanai, Burrell Boom, Sand Hill, Ladyville, Caye Caulker, Guadalupe, Maskall, and St. Ann's. She has visited them all frequently. Now, however, she says, she is cutting back. At that time, she was still going twice a week to Sand Hill, only because "it had been dormant." She was trying to revive it. She said that she would go to the others in preparation for First Communion and Confirmation.

Describing her ministry, she told me that in each case she works through the school for two reasons: (1) the schools are a good avenue to families; (2) most of the schools need help. She could be of assistance to the teachers. "The people need to be nourished," she added.

She said, regretfully, "The teacher's house in Rancho was vacant. A family from St. Ann's parish is renting it. Places like this are available. A group could live in one of those houses and feed into Bermudian Landing."

I left Josella that day, understanding why Father Cull, SJ, had called her "Apostle of the Road." We have met her previously in Chapter Five, where we found her just as much an apostle on the pastoral team in San Ignacio, as she was an apostle of the road in Belize City.

Sister Josella had included Maskall on her list of villages. Bob Olvey, SJ, a member of the faculty of St. John's College who served the parish at Maskall, said that a small group of people of deep faith lived there. Others, he said, are greatly in need of help in the practice of their faith. He expressed the wish that there might be a group of Belizeans similar to the Jesuit International Volunteers (JIV) and more people like Sister Josella and Martina Bardalez. Anyone who knows Martina can understand why Father Olvey would like to see her "multiplied." I first knew Martina as a member of the lay ministers of the Belize District when they met at St Ignatius in the early eighties. As for Belizean JIVs, recently such a group has been organized, Jesuit Volunteers Belize (JVB), with Carolee Chanona, RSM, as program director.

Eileen Hannon, OP, who succeeded Elizabeth Miles as Director of the Lay Ministry Program, had very kindly arranged for me to meet a group of those ministers during that October '91 visit. I presented to that group of forty-five women and men, most of whom I had known for nearly a decade, our plan to work out of centers into the villages, and I asked their honest opinion.

Their response was a wholehearted, "Yes!" They saw it as an antidote to the takeover, as they called it, by the new churches. One man said, "Even my mother-in-law has joined them. She says, 'I'm not gonna sit around for weeks and months waiting for a priest to come. These people are here!'" They mentioned the need for Spanish-speaking people in some villages, the need for Spanish-speaking lay ministers. The entire discussion was heartening, very encouraging.

I had hoped to talk with Bishop Martin before leaving Belize, but he had to go out of town at that time. Reviewing the meeting I had had with him just after my arrival, I was confident that he would be happy with the results of the month's survey. I recalled that when I talked with him he had before him the letter I had written explaining our proposal.

"Your main idea seems to be increased presence," he said, and added, "I do believe in presence to the people." He spoke appreciatively of the ministry of the Madrecitas in the Orange Walk District.

They live with the people, three weeks at a time, three or four times a year. "That is what I used to do," he said, "when I was associate pastor in Orange Walk and in Cayo."

When we discussed the places that had been suggested as centers, I told him about Sister Barbara's suggesting that we consider Independence and that we talk with Beth Zabaneh about it. He approved of that. Had he been free to meet with me at the end of the month, I would have told him that we had had that meeting, that Beth had brought a sizeable group from the village, and that we had had a very enlightening discussion. I would have told him of my visits to Belize Rural and about how much I had learned in those visits. All of those developments I reported to him later by mail.

As I left Belize that time, it seemed that everything was pointing toward the village of Independence, and so it was. I was satisfied, even enthusiastic about Independence, but there has continued in my heart a hope that some day we may go also to the area called Belize Rural to work with people like Jane and Faustino.

Lingering in my heart also is the hope that some day we may resume the kind of ministry we used to pursue in the heart of the City. I know that we have tried to respond with the numbers that we have to the needs that are greatest. It seems to me, however, that the ministers in the City could assist greatly with ministry in the rural areas if they were introduced to the needs there and to the ways that they might help. They have the ability, the education, and the experience.

Early on, as they say in Massachusetts, I promised myself that I would be very objective in this effort to present our mission in Belize. I think that I have kept that promise so far. Today, however, I happened upon a 1990 edition of *SCN Mission News*. There I found a poem that I had written after my visit described above. It is a part of that visit and must be included. By way of introduction I said, "Even though the Spirit is moving us toward the villages, our experience in Belize City, Dangriga, and San Ignacio is close to our hearts."

Caribbean City,
you grip me,
entwine yourself around me,
become so much a part of me
I begin to move according to your rhythm,
hardly aware that I am traipsing over sand
and potholes, mud, and rocks and dirt.
Rays of sun beat down relentlessly, but only
in my subconscious do I sense their filtered heat.

Walking, walking, walking
mile after mile,
my feet tread lightly on these roads
that lead me to something, somewhere,
or someone.

There is a map;
I know there is.
I know this journey's not haphazard,
even though I move without apparent destination.
At end of day,
washing my dusty feet,
I remember smiles, tears,
and many a warm embrace.
Are these what draw me on and on,
making obstacles along the way seem not to be?

Yes . . .
but still it seems there's something else,
something about to happen,
as if sometime when I look down to avoid a pool
left by last night's rain,
I'll look up suddenly and see
that sparkle of the sun upon the sea
has washed over the land,

removing the layer of roughness,
and leaving only the beauty that is really there.

Is this the fascination:
so much beauty
hidden only from those
who cannot see?

Experience has told me that some lovers of prose consider writers of verse to be impractical people. In defense of "poets" then, this chapter closes with a very practical suggestion. Clement Wade, long-time Superintendent of Schools in Belize, in stressing the need for increased health care in the villages, told me that good teachers in elementary schools in the States make excellent ministers of health care in the villages of Belize. Health as taught in elementary schools of America, he said, is exactly what is needed.

Chapter Fifteen

MOVEMENT SOUTH: TOLEDO DISTRICT

Before continuing the story of Independence, it is important to find out what had been going on for a long time in the southernmost part of the country. The romantically inclined who expect to find a connection between the Toledo District in Belize and the city of Toledo in Spain will be disappointed. It was so named by a group of people from Toledo, Ohio, who, sometime in the early 1900s, found the spot, liked it, and settled there. Oral history tells that gradually others joined them. When the settlement became large enough to require a name, the people requested of the government the name Toledo.

No one objected, so Toledo it became. When Belize was included in the SCN program *Justice '75*, SCNs Kitty Wilson and Rose Mary Gerlica were assigned to San Antonio, a Maya-Mopan village in the Toledo District. There they were asked to take a census, an assignment requiring that they visit every home in the area. Their reports reveal the value of that experience. They met the Maya people, who welcomed them graciously, supplied the information they had been asked to gather, and made each visit something they soon began to anticipate with joy and now remember with heartfelt gratitude.

Twenty-five years later Kitty recalls one of the events of that assignment. Eleven-year-old Clementi Bol asked her to accompany

In a middle-class home in the village, a mother prepares supper for her three children. The children keep her busy, for she continues to cook on the little stove at the table.

him to the home of some of his relatives five miles "back in the bush" from San Antonio. Kitty followed him as he cleared the way for her. They spent the day talking with his relatives about village life and watching people collect honey and make tortillas and corn wine. As Kitty and Clementi were leaving, the people gave her a jar of honey, in keeping with Mayan custom of always presenting a guest with a gift; and the Alcalde, leader of the village, said, "Sis Kitty, if you come back and teach us the Bible and explain to us what it means, we'll make a road so you won't have to walk."

On the way back to San Antonio Village, Kitty and Clementi climbed a very high hill, a veritable mountain it seems. There they thanked God for the beautiful experience of the day and for the magnificence of the surrounding country. As they descended the hill, however, they realized that they were not sure of which way to turn and it was growing dark. Kitty recalled accounts that she had heard of people wandering in those hills for three days, trying to find their way out. Looking for someone to direct them, they realized that they had not passed anyone who might give them directions, but, just as they were beginning to grow fearful, they saw a man tending a garden not far from the hill. When they approached him and asked for directions, he pointed out a creek nearby.

"Just follow the creek," he said, " it will take you to San Antonio."

"I was so relieved," says Kitty, "that I didn't wonder immediately how he happened to be there to direct us. When I did look back, he was nowhere in sight. To this day I am convinced that he was Jesus, caring for us and guiding us." Kitty continues:

> That whole summer was filled with good experiences. Rose Mary Gerlica and I visited every home in San Antonio. We made a map of the entire village, locating every home, all the roads, and the path to every house. We talked with the people, especially the mothers of families. Most of the fathers were out in the fields working. The pastor, Jack Ruoff, SJ, knew his people well, but he wanted us to find out their needs. We were able to do that during those weeks, and the people were very grateful. Even several years later our map was still on the wall in the rectory. It had proved helpful, and they were proud of it.

Maria Sanchez was one of the young people who benefited from that summer. Here we find her writing her name for the first time.

Kitty completed her *Justice '75* summer in San Antonio. After a year at home in the States, she returned to Belize, that time to Dangriga for two years, then to San Ignacio for two years. Those four years were spent as teacher, consultant for teachers of religion, and as director of programs for youth, including youth retreats. She left Belize in 1980.

Justice '75 extended to the following summer, when among those participating were Kitty's sister, Carolyn Wilson, SCN, and Martha Clan, SCN. They took up the census work that Kitty and Rose Mary had begun, taking it to nearby towns. Carolyn remembers feeling that they were living in a jungle. There was a great deal of flooding that summer, but they managed both teaching and census-taking. They recall that one day when Jack Ruoff was not able to drive them, they started to walk the several miles to the school. To their surprise, the children met them halfway.

In 1991 Kitty returned to Belize, at the request of Barbara Flores, then Director of Religious Education there, who had asked her to write a text for use in instruction for the Sacrament of Confirmation. Kitty had agreed to do so on condition that, in preparation, she visit teachers and students in all six districts of the country.

Kitty spent six months visiting schools, getting responses from teachers and students in order to know their needs and their special interests with regard to the Sacrament. Those visits were enjoyable as well as instructive; one was especially so. When she visited San Pedro Columbia, she found Clementi, her friend of that summer of 1975. Now a fine young man, married and father of two, he was teaching the fourth grade. He greeted her warmly. "Sis," he cried, "you drank the water! You did come back!"

Then, "Sis, come meet my children!" He introduced her to his class, and she sensed immediately that he had an excellent rapport with the children. To her delight, he was also one of the teachers of religion with whom she was scheduled to work.

Not everyone who ministers in Belize or anywhere else in the world has such a simple yet unusual experience as Kitty had with

Clementi. Many do experience generally, however, the joy of seeing the results of their efforts and of knowing how God has blessed those efforts.

Stories of ministry in the Toledo District from 1975 to 1994 merit a volume of their own. A summary of them cannot do them justice, but a brief review of them is essential to a grasp of Belize/SCN relationship.

First acquaintance with cultures other than one's own tends to create an awareness of differences. Even among those differences, however, there are always similarities that spark relationships. Martha Clan, SCN, says, "San Antonio will always have a special place in my heart. Carolyn Wilson and I walked each day, taking census and teaching Bible School in Manfredi. On those walks we were in awe of the beauty of the hillside, the mountain, the small creek

SCN Brenda Gonzales and the women of her adult reading class in San Pedro stop after class to talk about preparing for the next lesson. Surely the seed of good reading skills is being planted in the minds of the little ones who attend class with their mothers.

where we took our bath, the same place where the people bathed and washed their clothes. The beauty of the people, the simplicity of their lifestyle will always have special meaning for me."

The special program *Justice '75* had extended to 1976. The program proper came to an end, but its purpose had been accomplished. SCNs had become acquainted with other countries, other cultures. Many had availed themselves of the opportunity of visiting Belize and of participating in ministry there. Many of those who did so consider themselves blessed by the experience.

Some of those experiences were laced with sadness. Caroline Field, who, with Mildred McGovern, spent a month in Silver Creek Village during the summer of 1979, tells of going to say "good-bye" to one of the families there. When she knocked at the door very early in the morning, Pablo, the father of the family, opened it quietly, saying, "My son was born dead this morning, and my wife may also be dying."

Caroline went over to the bed of the mother, where the father's mother was caring for her. There was a fire burning beside the bed. Both mother and grandmother began to cry quietly when they saw her.

"Nothing seemed real," says Caroline, "my words seemed empty. Pablo brought me the baby, wrapped like a papoose. He handed me a coke bottle filled with water and asked me to baptize the baby. It was impossible to find a priest, so surrounded were we by flood waters."

After the baptism, Pablo asked Caroline to conduct the funeral. No one in the village came. It was considered a curse for a baby to be born dead because of its being too late for baptism. Caroline says:

> So, with Pablo leading the way, Sister Millie and I, together with the couple's five-year-old son and a seven-year-old niece, formed a procession and walked slowly into the jungle where Pablo had dug a grave. By the time the procession reached the grave, it had filled with water. While Pablo dipped the water out, the little boy began to sing "He's got the whole world in

his hands." The lines, "He's got the itty bitty baby in his hands" brought tears and sobs to the little band of mourners.

Finally, at the father's signal, I lowered the papoose into the mud. While Pablo struggled within himself for courage to shovel mud into the grave, we sang *Kum ba yah*. Gradually, he covered his son's grave shovel by shovel, and the funeral procession returned to the home.

That was a sad closing to an otherwise joyful summer experience. Many happy memories remain, however, as when Millie recalls "swimming near the coral reef among the tropical fish in clear water that reflected the blue sky."

The SCNs did not begin until 1982 to live and work in the Toledo District full time. Carmella Vargas of Dangriga had completed her education to become a nurse practitioner. The Government, seeing the need to expand health care in the south, placed Carmella in Dangriga, in the position formerly held by Anna Marie Nalley, and directed the latter to San Antonio. That was the same year that SCNs

This funeral procession of a child resembles the one described above only insofar as the body of a beloved child is being taken to its final resting place. Here the family is obviously in better circumstances and their sorrow not intensified by mistaken beliefs.

Mary Lynn Fields and Mary Ransom Burke opened the mission in Belize City. *SCN Mission News,* in the spring of that year, remarked that San Antonio was the fourth SCN mission to be established in Belize, the others being Dangriga, San Ignacio, and Belize City.

That same publication reported the commissioning of sixteen men and women in St. Peter Claver Church in Punta Gorda on February 14, 1982. "That was the Toledo District's first commissioning," it stated. According to that article the Pallottine Sisters of the parish hosted the SCNs, the Holy Family Sisters, and the Sisters of Mercy who attended the ceremony. The ministry of the laity was developing throughout Belize. From Toledo in the south through Corozal in the north, men and women were responding to call of Vatican II.

It was the Madrecitas from Mexico who led the program in Orange Walk and Belize's northernmost districts. the *Christian Herald,* publication of the Catholic Diocese of Belize, in its November 1979 issue, featured the dedication of the first convent of that religious community in Belize. Known officially as the Missionary Daughters of the Holy Mother of Light, the sisters came from Merida to Belize at the invitation of Carlos Franco, a priest of the diocese, to work among the Spanish-speaking people in the villages of the Orange Walk District. Bishop Martin speaks enthusiastically of their ministry. They engage primarily in catechetical instruction and the training of catechists to carry on the work in their own villages. According to the *Christian Herald*, "A normal schedule finds two of the sisters at work as a small band, staying in any particular village for three weeks' time (p. 9)."

Some people whom we have interviewed have pointed out that staying in the villages for several days at a time or for several weeks has advantages over going in for a day at a time. The Madrecitas have demonstrated that value. Each group of religious works according to its particular style and plan.

When Anna Marie went to San Antonio in 1982, she took up residence in a small house opposite the parish church of San Luis Rey. Some time later the priests announced that they were moving to

Punta Gorda, twenty miles away, from which they would commute to San Antonio twice a week, Sundays and one other day. The scarcity of priests was becoming evident. "It's an ill wind that blows no good," however. When they were leaving, the priests suggested that the sisters take over the rectory for use as a convent, a suggestion that proved providential. Gradually the convent was filled, first by a local community of SCNs and one Dominican sister, then more than filled periodically by SCNs and another Dominican sister, all of whom came from the other missions for weekend meetings. There were no rooms for the latter, but there were plenty of nooks and crannies for the cots borrowed from the British army that was still guarding the Belize-Guatemala border.

The eighties was a period of much coming and going in that southernmost area of Belize. Previous to Anna Marie Nalley's placement by the Government Health Services, no SCNs had been in permanent residence there. As interesting and as productive as had been those six-week summer stints, they had been all too short.

Soon after Anna Marie moved to the new residence, which had been the old rectory, she was joined by SCN Philomena Kottoor from India. A student in the Department of Nursing at Spalding University, Philomena spent her spring break in Belize assisting Anna and gaining in-service education.

Soon after Philomena had returned to Louisville, Ransom had a call from the Belize City Hospital informing her that Anna had become seriously ill while in Crique Sarco and had been transported by plane to Belize City.

Joan Dunning, OP, who was having supper at the SCN house in Belize City, accompanied Ransom to the hospital. By the time they reached there, whatever had been Anna Marie's physical problem had lessened considerably but had remained undiagnosed. For several weeks she was transferred from place to place, hoping each time for a diagnosis.

Ransom was the only SCN in Belize City; Lynn had gone to the States to study. The house was fully occupied, however, by sisters of another community who had come for the summer to assist in ministry. The Sisters of Mercy invited Anna Marie to St. Catherine's, where she stayed a few days until another attack of the illness required hospitalization once more. That time the doctor recommended the one private hospital in the City, where he hoped special tests could find the cause of the illness. After several days there, however, it became evident that Anna Marie would have to go to the States.

The Sisters of Mercy came to the rescue once more. While Ransom tracked down Sarah Ferriell, SCN, who was conducting Bible school in places hard to reach by phone, and SCN Maria Vincent Brocato, Southern Provincial, the Sisters of Mercy made arrangements with their hospital in New Orleans to admit Anna Marie. Fortunately, Maria Vincent was visiting relatives in Tennessee. She flew immediately to New Orleans to meet Anna there. Marian Joseph Baird, RSM, who had generously joined Lynn temporarily in 1975 and who by 1982 was preparing for a career in nursing, advanced travel plans made for the following week in order to accompany Anna Marie, who traveled on a stretcher. The emergency airline reservations were obtained by Caritas Lawrence, a Sister of Mercy, some of whose former students worked in the office of the airline. Examination indicated the need for more extended hospitalization. Return to the strenuous work in Belize was not advised. Evidently, Anna Marie's gift to Belize was meant for Stann Creek District from 1976 to 1982 and for San Antonio from 1982 to 1983.

Ann Moyalan, who came from India to assist Anna Marie, found herself taking Anna's place. Fortunately Ann was well prepared to manage it all. In the Winter 1983 issue of the *SCN Mission News,* Ann is quoted:

> I started work in the San Antonio clinic from the 31st of October. By the end of November the rural health nurses here will be transferred and I will have to manage the clinic here as well as a few mobile clinics in the surrounding villages. . . . I've signed the contract for 2 years with the government. This place and the clinic remind me of Chaibasa [in India]. We do

Clinic Day at Blue Creek. SCN Ann Moyalan serves the children and talks with the mothers about how to keep the little ones healthy.

prenatals, well baby clinics, out patients, deliveries, post natals, home visits, school health, mobile clinics, community participation, etc. In Anna's absence I help with the community health workers training programme. There are 5 under this center. (p. 7)

It is evident that by the time Ann wrote that summary of her job description she had that job well under control. One cannot help considering how providential it was that the SCN chosen to *assist* Anna was one who had the credentials and the experience to take the place Anna had to leave. From the perspective of a community in mission, there is evidence, also, of the hand of Providence in that Sister Ann from India replaced Sister Anna from the United States to care for people of Belize. In that change there is evidence too that the SCN mission in India had matured sufficiently to reach out to our young mission in Belize.

Chapter Sixteen

MIXED MESSAGES:
PLEASE STAY; GO, OR ELSE

W hile Ann was finding her way into this new venture, John Loretto Mueller, SCN, was arriving. She landed in Belize City in the midst of heavy rain with very heavy baggage, mostly supplies for the mission. Lynn and Ransom met her at the International Airport and took her and her baggage to Maya Airways for the flight to Toledo. JL, as she is fondly called, and the other passengers boarded the plane, and the baggage was duly loaded on. The pilot did his best to get the plane into the air, but the soggy sand refused to comply. JL's baggage was removed; the pilot did a limited takeoff, proving wherein lay the problem. He suggested that we take the baggage to the International Airport, assuring us that it would be accommodated there.

"If baggage is transported within the country from International, might a passenger accompany her baggage?" we asked.

Being assured that she might, we boarded JL and her baggage on our little Ford truck and set out once more for International. The old adage, "'Tis an ill wind that blows no good," proved the goodness of the wind that day. We had a visit with JL on the way from airport to airport that we would not have had otherwise. Her arrival in San Antonio, the little village in Toledo where Ann awaited her, was confirmed that night by telephone, the one telephone in the village at that time.

A little later Ann wrote: "John Loretto works with the parish team and the teachers. Both of us are finding our way around. People are friendly, call us, greet us, smile at us, so there is much hope."

Joan Dunning, OP, who had been visiting Ransom when they received word of Anna's illness, was at that time in the health ministry in Toledo. By the time Ann and JL arrived, however, she had been transferred elsewhere by the Belize Department of Health. What a boon it would have been to Ann to have had Joan for an orientation.

Undaunted, however, Ann wrote, "Both of us have a good community life and feel supported by the other SCNs in Belize. Ours is a natural life style—kerosene lamp and moonlight for the night, rain or well water for drinking and washing purposes. Life is going on smoothly and I am learning to love it" (*SCN Mission News*, Winter 1983, p. 9).

Writing in January 1985, John Loretto said, "Today SCN Irene Locario arrived. We now have an unusual community—really

Higinia Bol entered the Novitiate of the Sisters of Charity at Nazareth, Kentucky, in the Fall of 1998. She made her vows there in August 2001. As this book goes to press, she is a member of the faculty of St. Martin de Porres School in Belize City. She is pictured here with her mother and father, Clemencia and Ponciano Bol.

international—Ann from India, Irene from Belize, and I from the US. Irene, recently professed as an SCN, came to teach in the elementary school." It was through her that Higinia Bol, who was teaching in that school, became acquainted with the Sisters of Charity of Nazareth. Several years later Higinia entered the novitiate at Nazareth, Kentucky. She made her profession as a member of the Community in August of the year 2001.

In the letter just quoted, January 1985, John Loretto mentions a number of times the visit of Dorothy MacDougall, SCN President, and the various meetings with her, including her attendance at the closing of the novena of Esquipulas, the black crucified Christ. According to the story, Christ appeared in that form to a group of slaves in Guatemala many years ago. The devotion is very important to the Indian people. It has long since crossed the border into Belize.

A letter the following year at Easter time was packed with news. It told of the cursillos (workshop-retreats) for the catechists. "After this week," says JL, "there are two more to go." Bishop Martin was expected in San Antonio for commissioning and recommissioning. According to that letter there was some improvement in roads. A few places that JL had not been able to reach by truck were becoming available in the dry season. The government was hiring the Mennonites to repair them.

In March of that year, according to the letter just quoted, JL took fifty-nine of the 118 Catechists to Belize City for the national gathering of Catechists. On Friday night when JL and a group of the young people were walking down a street in Belize City, they were stopped by the police, who asked how they had gotten into the country. When they explained very calmly that they had been born in Belize, the police were surprised and a bit embarrassed. It is hard, even for the police, to keep up with ethnic variety in Belize. Later that night they met the same policemen who, this time, stopped traffic and showed them across the street.

One other story in that letter of Easter, 1986, warrants inclusion for several reasons. First, those of us who have spent time in Belize can account for its being unusual. Second, it demonstrates the possibility of accomplishing the impossible. Third, it is a whopping good story. By that I do not mean that it is only a story. It is a true one.

JL says, "On Thursday, Father Thro and I had a first-time experience with Jalacte [pronounced *halak'tay*], our newest village," located about a half-mile from the Guatemala border. JL said that at that time the best way to get there was by helicopter. They might have arranged for that, but it would have meant walking home, and that would have been impossible.

Father Thro told the Catechists there, who were begging them to come, to find two horses and two leather saddles. The Catechists in Jalacte found two mules and two saddles, so off on their first ride went Bill Thro and JL early in the morning of February 13, 1986. Granted, Bill and JL were many years younger than they are today, but even then they were, shall we say, mature.

JL says that the beginning was not bad. There were about two miles of good road before they had to go into "high bush that never dries out." She says: "We traveled up, up, up and down, down, down, nine huge hills, lying practically flat coming down and leaning forward as far as possible going up hill." They finally made it and had a good visit. It was the return trip that had snags. "It wasn't enough," says JL, "that the ground was soft and wet! We got caught in a blinding rain. A horse would have been bogged down, but mules are cautious animals."

Many people reading her letter knew JL well, and knew that riding a horse had been a favorite sport of hers before she entered the community. She had been learning to jump and had gotten up to three feet. Writing of those days, she says, "I once paid a lot to ride a horse. This time I would have paid double for the ride to come to an end. About a half-mile before we got to the good road, Padre dropped from his mount. After resting for about ten minutes, he remounted and we started for home once again."

Thinking that all was going well, JL relaxed. "I was letting the mule find the best place to step," she said, "when a huge vine caught me under the chin. I thought for sure my turn to drop had come. I was parallel to the horse's back when at the last millionth of a second the vine snapped and I was able to proceed in safety."

Although JL is an accomplished horsewoman, that was her first experience of riding without a bit and bridle. She says, "I just had one rope to hold on to. Coming back, we had to hold onto the backs of our saddles so that we wouldn't slip off because of the rain and the mud. Did we appreciate this experience? You bet we did! We plan on going again, but with no short cuts included."

Another account of an experience in the Toledo District appeared a few months later in *SCNews*. Involved were Jane Karakunnel, SCN; Mary Otho Ballard, OP; Amina Bejos, SCN; and Higinia Bol. Jane, like Ann Moyalan, had come from India to participate in the new Belizean mission. Mary Otho, like Elizabeth Miles and Joan Dunning, is a Dominican from St. Catherine, Springfield, Kentucky, neighbor to Nazareth. At that time she was in Belize temporarily, to return two years later for a ministry of five years. Amina was, at that time, an SCN novice and Higinia, a lay teacher, later to become an SCN.

JL left and Marian Joseph Baird, RSM, use the prevailing mode of travel in the hills of Cayo. Their journey, however, returning from a cursillo, is less eventful than the one described in our story.

The four of them went to Crique Sarco, a remote village in the Toledo District, to conduct a Bible school. Jane is quoted as saying, "July fifth started with heavy rain and storms in contradiction to predictions." In order to reach Crique Sarco from San Antonio they had to go to the coastal town of Punta Gorda and then travel through the Caribbean and the Temash River for about four and a half hours. They waited for the rain to stop, but getting to the highway in order to reach Punta Gorda was difficult because parts of the highway were flooded. They did reach Punta Gorda, however, and when the rain stopped, the four and one half hours on the water were delightful. When they arrived at Crique Sarco, they received a very warm welcome, especially from the children who were eager to have classes. They had class only three days a week during the school year.

According to Amina, the teachers worked with an average of forty-five children a day, ages four to thirteen. Amina taught them music and arts and crafts; Jane, Bible stories; and Mary Otho and Higinia, Bible stories and dramatization. Evidently those were happy classes.

Jane says that during the day the men went to the plantations while the women did the housework. In the evenings the "four" visited families and got acquainted with their simple way of life and with their culture generally. "I am very much impressed by the faith of the people," she said. "They come together as a family to worship and to play. They are poor, hard working, simple, and friendly. They are the *anawim* of *Yahweh*, the lowly ones of the *Magnificat*. They are rich in simplicity, love, hospitality, rituals—in a particular culture generally."

At seven o'clock each night the sisters showed two reels of Zeffirelli's film, *Jesus of Nazareth*. This did not conflict with the home visits. In Belize, evening begins at three o'clock and ends at seven. After that it is night. Amina said that practically everyone in the village came to the showings. "At the sound of the generator," she said, "they left their homes."

On Sundays and Wednesdays the sisters conducted communion service with the catechists. The church was filled every time, and the visitors found the liturgy in the Ketchi language and the ritual truly inspiring. Jane said, "I became more and more aware of the universality and uniqueness of the Church and of myself as a Catholic, an SCN, and an Indian (from India)."

Jane had planned to return to San Antonio at the end of the first week in order to help John Loretto prepare for the commissioning of the Catechists (ministers). By that time, however, the river was high and the sea very rough. When the British soldiers on duty there heard of her plight, they offered to take her in their boat. After an hour on the river, the boat's motor refused to function. The soldiers immediately contacted headquarters, and, says Jane, "I had my first helicopter ride."

Jane arrived in San Antonio in time to assist with the preparation of the catechists. Two years later, Thomas Rochford, SJ, described for the *Jesuit Bulletin*, Fall 1988, page 6, part of one of those sessions. He pictures for the reader Juan Chee "listening to a lecture given by Jane Karakunnel." He explains who Jane is and that she has come from India to do pastoral work in Belize with another Sister of Charity of Nazareth, John Loretto. He explains that they form the pastoral staff for twenty-seven villages.

An account of the commissioning was in *SCNews* for September 1986, reporting that on July 20 in San Antonio village, Toledo District, one hundred five Maya and Ketchi Indians (ninety-seven men and eight women) were commissioned as catechists. The inclusion of women was "a first," a real break with tradition. Their year's training program included (1) three week-long training sessions in Guatemala conducted by teacher-catechists under Jane's supervision, (2) attendance at the Ministers Gathering in Belize City, and (3) a two-day retreat directed by Belizean priest, Callistus Cayetano, immediately before the commissioning.

Those Maya teachers were trilingual, speaking Mopan and Ketchi as well as English. Some of the participants had to walk for as many as eleven hours because no transportation was available at that time. The British Army personnel transported all the catechists to San Antonio for the July 18-20 weekend and back to their villages afterwards.

At the commissioning Mass, conducted in both English and Ketchi, each catechist received a certificate, a cross, and a Sunday missal provided by a grant from the Jesuits. Each of the twenty-nine villages received a Bible in the Maya or Ketchi language. Jane soon initiated a training program in San Antonio for preparation of catechists, making it unnecessary for them to take the long trek to Guatemala.

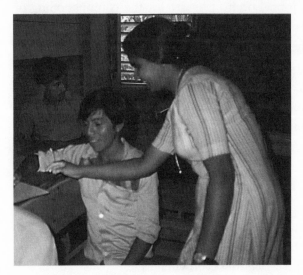

SCN Jane Karakunnel is helping the young man improve the essay that he has written. He is one of those being commissioned as a lay minister.

The main thrust of the Rochford story quoted above is the development of the "new Church." Rochford contrasts the Church of 1851, the Church of strong individuals such as Jesuit Bishops Frederick C. Hopkins and Salvatore Di Pietro, and of the Jesuit missionary priest, William Stanton in 1905, with the Church of today in which so much depends on women religious and lay ministers. Rochford writes objectively, giving credit where it obviously belongs at the time at which the events occur in the history of the Church.

The church of San Luis Rey, where the commissioning took place, is very large, surprisingly so, until one recalls that there is only one Mass on Sunday, and that there are hundreds of Maya families living in the thatched huts that surround the imposing edifice. With the supervision of those early Jesuits, the church was built by the people, who carried the stones from the neighboring hillside. The cathedral-like height made it possible to accommodate stained glass windows from a church in St. Louis, Missouri, that had been razed. Visitors are surprised to see on those windows inscriptions in German and to be

Irene Locario renews her vows in the very large church—San Luis Rey. Witnessing the renewal are SCNs Adeline Ferhibach and Ann Kernen. Celebrant of the Mass at which the renewal ceremony takes place is Bill Thro, SJ, seated at right during the ceremony.

The height of the church can be visualized by noting that the archways on the ground floor are twice as high as the people standing under them.

*Jane Karakunnel,
SCN, is standing
beside the young
man being
commissioned
by Bishop Martin.
Witnessing the
ceremony is
Jack Ruoff, SJ.*

asked, in that language, to pray for the donor and the departed, both
identified as citizens of St. Louis. Yet, after all, it *is* the Church of *San
Luis* Rey.

To sit in that church built with stones carried across the border
by stalwart, loving hands of people seeking freedom of worship is to
experience something of that people's strength. As I sat there alone
one afternoon during one of my many visits to Toledo, I was
reminded of another structure, Xunantunich, my favorite Mayan
ruin in San Ignacio, built by pre-Christian ancestors of this people.
That ruin and this church hold a very true relationship imbedded in
the soul of a people.

Whatever may be the history of the stained-glass windows, there
is an unusual side altar to the right of the main altar, where we would
expect to find an altar in honor of St. Joseph. I call it an altar because
it is dedicated to several saints. It might be called more properly a collection of saints, for it consists of several images of varying heights,
two to three-and-a-half feet, within an enclosure. Whatever may be

the artistic value of the carvings, they are relics of a people who so valued religious freedom that they took images of their saints from San Luis Peten in Guatemala and carried them over the border into Belize as they marched into their new country for the sake of that freedom. San Antonio is built on that kind of foundation. It is not surprising, then, to witness the commissioning of one hundred five descendants of those pioneers in the church that the pioneers built.

It was good to be recalling Belizean pioneers in 1986 as SCNs looked forward to celebrating in 1987 the one hundred seventy-five years since their founding by descendants of people who had "marched" from Maryland to Kentucky in the late eighteenth century seeking freedom to practice their religion. On February 14, 1987, all SCNs in Belize celebrated that anniversary. There would be other celebrations, especially at Nazareth and in Louisville on the official date, December 1. It was important to those in Belize, however, to have a special celebration there. The particular date in Belize was chosen because Emily Nabholz, Southern Provincial, and Josephine Barrieau, SCN, Director of SCN Missions, were visiting at that time. Jane, John Loretto, and Irene went to Dangriga to join with all the others for the event.

After the celebration, the entire group of SCNs left for San Antonio. Barbara Flores, who was then director of religious education in Belize, had planned to come, but the serious illness of her father took her to Honduras instead. All the others participated in a three-day gathering. It was an eventful meeting. Amina Bejos, novice, shared with the group her desire to become a vowed member of the Congregation. All approved her doing so and offered their prayerful support. "On the last day of the meeting," states the *Annals of San Antonio,* "we all shared how we were implementing the resolutions of the Guatemala meeting of the previous September."

Succeeding months witnessed steady ministry in the midst of change. When Barbara Flores returned from her father's funeral, she visited San Antonio before leaving for the States to study. Soon Irene would also be leaving for the purpose of continuing her education.

Annals give evidence of progress in the Catechist/Lay Ministry Program. In March of 1988 John Loretto and Jane accompanied forty-two catechists to Corozal for the third National Gathering of Lay Ministers. Jane's commitment of two years in Belize was coming to a close. Before she left August 25, gatherings of ministers and of the youth group that she had organized expressed genuine appreciation of what that commitment had meant to them. One of the young people said, "When Sister Jane left, the youth in San Antonio cried in their hearts."

A few days later Elaine McCarron, SCN, a specialist in the teaching of religion, arrived to spend three months of her sabbatical assisting teachers in the Catholic schools of Belize. Elaine was, at the time, a consultant in education for the bishops of the United States. In October Elaine gave a three-day workshop for teachers. She was assisted by Adeline Fehribach, SCN, from Dangriga, who held sessions on homiletics.

Immediately after the workshop, Elaine traveled through the south with Ben Juarez, District Manager of Schools, to assist teachers in implementing some of the plans developed during those three days. During much of that time she stayed with JL in San Antonio. Meanwhile Jean Kulangara from India had joined John Loretto temporarily. Sister Paschal Maria joined them in October.

In May 1990, John Loretto returned to Kentucky. She had been in ministry in Belize six and a half years. Shortly before leaving, she was invited to a Palm Sunday liturgy at Pueblo Viejo. Today, a decade later, she recalls that liturgy with deep emotion.

"Palm Sunday is a big day with the Mayas," she says. "There is the blessing of palms and readings, followed by Mass if it is the priest's day to be there, otherwise by a prayer service, then the Deer Dance and a big feast." At one point the catechist for that day called JL to the podium where a representative of each village presented her with a farewell gift. In addition, the older women of the villages took turns putting monetary gifts in the cuxtal that she had on her shoulder.

During that recent interview with JL, I asked her for other memories of that southernmost district of Belize. She has a wealth of them, many involving Sisters Ann Moyalan and Jane Karakunnel. Reminding me that Ann had seventeen villages to cover, she recalled the help that it had been to have the British Army encamped at Salamanca, three miles from San Antonio.

"There was a change of command every six months," she recalled, "and we educated each new regiment, explaining particular characteristics of the area. When the deep south villages would be cut off from us by flooding, we would 'get a drop' when they went in for their men by helicopter.

"One day, when Ann was being assisted by the army, they came to a flooded river. One of the officers tethered to the other side tied a rope to a huge tree, and Ann, along with the soldiers, crossed the river by swinging on the rope."

JL recalls one of many serious cases to which Ann Moyalan was called. The Pablo Chun family had a baby one week old. Late one night, in answer to a knock at the door, Ann went with Pablo to his house where the baby was suffering with a high fever. Ann baptized the baby and stayed with the family all night, doing mouth-to-mouth resuscitation. Ann taught the mother the procedure, and between them the baby survived.

"Early in the morning Pablo went for the priest to baptize the baby," says JL, "the second baptism." JL continued, "With our Indian people, bells are to be rung after baptisms, weddings, and funerals so, as you might have guessed, after Ann and the parents came up with the mighty name of Samson, the third baptism counted and everyone was invited for caldo, corn tortillas, coke, and sweet coffee."

JL spoke of the youth group that Jane had formed, calling it countercultural among the Maya people. She said that Jane's experience with youth in India had prepared her well. "Up to today," says JL, "the Indian youth in Belize are benefiting from that experience. It can be observed in relationships. There are even some choices in marriages."

JL's vivid memory of development among the Maya reminded me of the many roles that she had played in that development. I asked her about her time as pastoral administrator of San Luis Rey. "Yes," she said, "that was while Callistus Cayetano, the pastor, was studying in Bogotá. Bill Thro came down from Belize City to serve in the Toledo District. He, Herb Panton, Josefina, SAC, Marian Joseph Baird, RSM, and I formed the Pastoral Team." This comment by JL is worthy of note. Without purporting to do so, it illustrates well the teamwork in Belize among various groups of religious: Jesuit Bill Thro, Herb Panton, a diocesan priest, Josefina, a Pallottine Sister, Marian Joseph Baird, a Sister of Mercy, and John Loretto, a Sister of Charity. We have met most of the group previously. Josefina Alamilla, SAC, appears to be a newcomer. She is, however, one of the quiet, very effective ministers, always available unless she is out of the country, representing her community on important business.

After JL left in 1990, Mary Otho Ballard, OP, who had been in ministry in Belize briefly in 1986, returned to San Antonio full time. She and Paschal Maria staffed the mission until July 1993. Her memory of those years relates especially to the Mayan people themselves. "In training catechists," she says, "we tried to help them to help their own people in their own language, encouraging appreciation of their own culture."

Mary Otho Ballard, OP

Mary Otho describes sessions in conflict resolution for the purpose of helping the people to resolve their differences. She recalls workshops for young people of high school age from a number of villages. She describes how Paschal Maria, SCN, worked with the women in making and marketing their special kind of baskets. In regard to the Catechists, Mary Otho says, "They knew who the wise ones were, the 'old heads' on whose thinking you could depend."

She recalls how well attended the cursillos were in Pueblo. "Pascal and I were celebrants at many funerals," she recalls, "and some of those funerals were very sad." She remembers one especially. She can still see the father and children in the candlelight around the casket of the mother. Mary Otho describes family rituals at harvest time with altars in the homes, candles at the four corners of the fields.

Then there was the Sunday when Mary Otho and two women took two priests, Ben Juarez and Callistus Cayetano, "back-a-bush" to begin "the walk" into the areas where there were no roads. Priests, religious, and lay ministers take this "walk" periodically to reach people to whom the Church would, otherwise, not be able to minister. After they had delivered their passengers, their truck stopped and refused to start again. Mary Otho stayed in the truck, and the two women went for assistance. It took them five hours, but they did return on a bus with help!

It was on another bus, ten years later, September 3, 2000, that I enjoyed hearing Mary Otho reminisce about her days in San Antonio. We were on our way to Dangriga from Belize City to celebrate the SCN Silver Jubilee there. When I urged her to continue, she spoke of how she and Paschal had encouraged the children to write poetry and to do needlework in just the way their ancestors had done. Adults were encouraged to participate in the arts, in the making of pottery, for example. She spoke of how well the men know the land, herbs, some medicines, and animals. They are even aware of which animals Queen Elizabeth especially likes. I learned one thing that day: a bus is an excellent site for an interview! The next and final episode of the story follows.

In January of 1993, opposition to the women religious began to surface. Families that had boarded young women who were completing their education under the tutelage of the sisters would no longer do so because of threats they had received. The sisters themselves received letters ordering them to leave the village or stay at the risk of their lives. They were not surprised. They had been aware of hidden opposition for some time. As is usually the case, it was a small, disgruntled group that was causing the difficulty. Some Belizean men do not like to see the women educated.

In February Mary Otho was invited to a village council meeting. She sent regrets, having heard about the manner in which those meetings were conducted. After the meeting, Pio Coc, one of the catechists, told her that a letter was being written to the Bishop and to the President of the Dominican congregation making clear the danger that was imminent. Pio advised the sisters that it was no longer safe to remain there.

The sisters made no hasty decisions. Rather they looked at plans they had already made for the future. Mary Otho had been planning to stay one more year. Paschal was expecting to go soon to the new mission just opening in Independence. That village, in the southernmost part of the Stann Creek District, is so close to the Toledo District, in which San Antonio is located, that Paschal knew that she could keep in touch with many of the people she would seem to be leaving.

As they were considering the whole situation and getting advice from people whom they trusted, the village council let it be known that it was responsible for their being asked to leave. How could a village council have so much power? What did that council have against the sisters?

It is not our purpose here to give a complete picture of Belize. The history of the country and its people has been well done by established historians, some of whose works are listed in the bibliography. To understand the problem with which we are currently concerned, however, it is necessary to understand something of the plan of local government. The national government, based on British law, is basically democratic. The prime minister is elected by the people of the six districts into which the country is divided. Within those districts, there are various styles of local management. Of those styles, says Narda Dobson, in her *History of Belize*, "the Alcalde system is perhaps the most interesting, as it is the only non-Anglo-Saxon institution in the country" (p. 291).

Dobson describes how those Maya, who came from Yucatan and Guatemala, introduced the Alcalde system and how it has been maintained in only the southern and western sections of the country. "The original system," she says, "was, at least superficially, very democratic. However, when this system was regularized and delimited by the government as late as 1952, it was almost inevitable that it should decline." By 1993 it had so declined in San Antonio that a few men were governing by means of fear tactics; and it had been proved that they really carried out their threats. People did have the right of recourse to district authority in Punta Gorda, a right, however, that was seldom exercised for fear of reprisal.

It was a new day, however. The very women whom the sisters had helped to find their true worth went to Punta Gorda, lodged a complaint against the village council and the Alcalde for exceeding their rights in forcing the sisters out of the village. Their case was taken all the way to Belmopan, where the court decided in favor of the women. The local leadership was disbanded and new elections initiated.

Although the people begged them to remain, the sisters chose to leave. Many felt that the culprits had become even more dangerous since they had been humiliated. Against that background, the courage of the women of San Antonio stands out even more boldly.

It is generally agreed that the intent of the missionary is to become unnecessary. Much remains to be done in San Antonio, much that the sisters could initiate and support. They left, however, confident that the Church there is in the hands of strong lay leaders.

The last cursillo of the year 1993 was held in Pueblo Viejo for the entire area. The annual commissioning took place at Mass offered by Bishop Martin. In his homily, the Bishop said that he had come for two reasons. One, he said, was a happy one, to commission the Catechists to take a much more active and responsible role among their villages. The other reason, he expressed sadly, was to say goodbye to the sisters who had worked so untiringly among them and had brought them to that point in ministry. He warned them "not to compare the sisters with the priests, because the sisters are women, who, therefore, are willing to do so much more than any man would do for them." The *Annals of San Antonio* state that "this drew smiles, nods, and applause, even from the Bishop."

That was nearly a decade ago. Many interested people still have many questions. SCNs and the Dominicans will always be welcomed by the people in the Toledo District, as the urgent plea of the women indicated. Who knows what the future may hold?

Chapter Seventeen

INDEPENDENCE:
A CENTER WITH OUTREACH

Place names have a way of sending the visitor to history. The previous chapter sent us looking for a relationship in Toledo, Spain, only to find it in Ohio, USA. If the title of this chapter elicits thoughts about the Fourth of July, or Independence Day, in the USA, we are reminded that other folk value freedom too. Legend has it that at the turn of the twentieth century people from several Central American countries, seeking a place to lead a peaceful life, settled in an area variously called *Big Creek* and *Mango Creek*. New arrivals settled in a place nearby and called it *Independence*.

"The founders" of these places can show a visitor the boundary lines of each one, as well as each one's special claim to fame. For example, Big Creek is really that, not much wider than a good-sized creek, but deep enough for ships to enter, anchor, accept a heavy load of bananas, and take off for Europe. A British produce company saw to that. Close by is Mango Creek, not navigable by ocean liners, but well able and very willing, for a fee, to carry groups of various sizes and ages across the lagoon to Placencia, a favorite vacation and picnic spot on the tip of a peninsula. Mango Creek serves also as a point of transfer to other places in the area, even to places such as Guatemala. Independence, while having neither port nor method of transport to pleasure, has a large elementary school and a high school that serve not only the immediate school population but also that of the surrounding area.

Each of the three—Big Creek, Mango Creek, and Independence—does its part, in those special ways, providing transportation or education. Measured in miles just off the Southern Highway, the three together do not take up much room on the map. It is not land that interests us here, however. Rather, it is the people—people who welcome us cordially and supply us with oral history beyond our most hopeful expectations. We knew that they would be friendly, for SCNs who had been in summer programs there for several years had found them so. Not surprising, for that has been SCN experience in every place that we have been in Belize in the last twenty-five years.

Theresa Murphy, SCN, recalls her summer in Mango Creek in the early eighties. Particularly alive is her memory of working with the children, "especially when they would come to our house each afternoon for storytelling, prayer, and singing.

"One family, the Monroys, often returned at night, since they lived close to us. They would bring with them their mother Mamirta. I used to hear from her, but I haven't heard lately," says Theresa.

The family's having moved from that area may account for the breakdown in correspondence. Not all members have moved, however. One of the older children, Curtis, now a young man and a teacher, was glad, at the time of our visit two years ago, to learn Sister Theresa's address. He wanted to send her an invitation to his wedding.

SCN Theresa Murphy recalls her summer in the early eighties, when "the children would come to our house every afternoon for storytelling, prayer, and singing."

The school building that had served for many years had just been replaced when we visited there in 1997. The Anglican-Roman Catholic agreement to cooperate in the operation of one elementary school had made it possible for the government to construct two strong buildings for the education of the children of the area. A similar arrangement had been made for the high school, which was operating successfully. The building that had housed the Catholic elementary school had served also for the church on Sundays when the priest from Dangriga would come for Mass, usually one, sometimes two Sundays a month. The building of the new school made it possible to tear down most of the old building, retaining only the room used as a church. That room, then, standing alone became the church. It was no larger than it had been; its appearance had not been enhanced at all, but it was a church rather than a room in a school, and that made a very great difference to the congregation.

Ever since that summer of *Justice'75*, when SCNs had gone in many directions for longer or shorter periods of time, a special relationship had been developing with Independence. The SCN Community had taken up residence in Dangriga, San Ignacio, San Antonio, and Belize City. The question of residence in Independence always remained open.

Chapter Fourteen recounts the SCN study in 1989-90 of where and how we might best serve Belize at that time. That chapter concludes with "everything pointing toward the village of Independence." At that time, SCN Amina Bejos lived in Dangriga and was manager of the Catholic schools in the Stann Creek District. Jean Turney, of the Jesuit International Volunteers, and SCN Mary Ransom Burke had joined her for the year 1989-90, Jean to direct the Lay Ministry Program, Ransom to assist them both.

On the Sundays when Jesuit Bill Thro offered Mass in one of the villages in the Independence area, Jean and Ransom would talk with the teenage group while the older people were gathering. The constant cry of the young people was, "We want sisters and priests who stay all week and teach us our religion."

Many of those young people were of refugee families from El Salvador, Guatemala, and Honduras. Pleasant amusement accompanied their attempts to understand our American Spanish and ours their attempted English. Genuine sincerity emerged on both sides, however, and the Americans tried to carry the message home. That message, brought to Nazareth at the time of the General Assembly of 1990, won strong encouragement. The meeting at which the message was discussed, however, was one of those addenda to assemblies that cover special topics, but carry no official sanction. An attempt to keep the interest alive throughout the following year continued by means of reports in *SCN Mission News.*

In the fall of 1991 I interviewed about fifty people in Belize, both Belizeans and Americans, ninety percent of whom confirmed the multiple needs listed at the 1990 discussion at Nazareth. Many agreed to assist if a mission should be established there.

Dialogue with Bishop Martin during the years 1991-1993 resulted in his enthusiastic support of the projected mission. He saw the need, however, to strengthen the pastorate in Dangriga, of which the church in Independence is a mission, before moving into a new program. That necessity was evident because the early nineties saw frequent changes among the clergy in Belize.

The parish in Dangriga was stabilized, however, when one of the Columban priests from Ireland became pastor. At the same time, as recounted in the previous chapter, the SCNs were withdrawing from San Antonio in the Toledo District, and Paschal Maria was planning to come from San Antonio to Independence. That made it possible to open the new mission while still keeping in touch with some of the women with whom Paschal had been working in San Antonio.

In the summer of 1993, Bishop Martin, with the assistance of Beth Zabaneh, had a house not far from the church remodeled to accommodate those who would administer the new mission. That house was the one in which Theresa Murphy had lived and in which she had held classes ten years earlier. In the fall of that year Paschal and Clara Cuellar, a young woman of Belize City who had volunteered

to assist her, moved into the house and began to become acquainted
with their neighbors, inviting them to join in their ministry.

In the summer of 1994, when Clara left to take a teaching position in the high school nearby, Sandy Sarangelo, a volunteer from
Ohio, joined Paschal for a period of seven months. Then, SCN Rosemarie Kirwan, who had served several short missions in Belize, the
last one in Independence in 1994, joined Paschal full time. During
my visit with them in 1997, they introduced me to their neighbors,
with whom I had many informal and very informative visits.

*SCNs Paschal Maria Fernicola and Rosemarie Kirwan have entertained
visitors in Independence. Besides enjoying cordial hospitality, those visitors
find it wise to break the journey from Belize City to the Toledo District and
on the return trip. Two of those visitors one time in 1994 were Miriam
Cannoit (left), volunteer worker with Guatemalan refugees in Chiapas,
Mexico; and Marciana (Chana) Funes, who organized the United Banners
Banana Workers' Union. Paschal (center) says, "thanks to her efforts and
struggles the living conditions of the workers are greatly improved."*

Independence has a history, but not of great discoveries, military campaigns, political movements, events that make the headlines. The history of Independence is written in the hearts of the people. The key to that history is conversation that includes listening to those hearts.

Those conversations are a privilege and a pleasure. It was easy to converse with Maria Conception Dolores Lourdes Chinchilla. She, who bears four titles of Mary of Nazareth, was born Christmas Eve 1903, twelve miles from Independence, at a place called Monkey River. She married Filadelfo Chinchilla December 8, 1928, and came to Independence. They had five children, three boys and two girls. She says, "My husband was a good man. We were married twenty years when he died in 1948."

When I saw her in 1997, she was busy writing to one of Belize's history buffs to fill him in on some of her early experiences and on the experiences of others in Independence. One of her happy memories is of two years in school at St. Catherine's Academy in Belize City.

One of her neighbors, Trudy Mena, also grew up twelve miles from Independence in Monkey River, where many people were employed by the United Fruit Company. "Miss Trudy" came to Independence with her husband and her one-month-old baby. She says that her husband has helped to build up the village. "People," she says, "began small and then expanded." Her family continues to use the well that they dug in 1963.

She recalls her early childhood when her father used to take the family up the river when school was out. They would wash clothes in the river and cook fish on the sand. When her father died, leaving five daughters, her uncle used to take them to the ship to sell things that their mother had made. She recalls too that their mother taught them to sew, and to make their clothes from material that cost twenty-five cents a yard.

Miss Trudy recalls midnight vigils when parishioners prayed throughout the night of December 7-8, feast of the Immaculate Conception, in the church in nearby Cowpen, a church that has since burned to the ground. "There would be shots at sunrise," she said, "a military salute to Mary, and music on accordions accompanying a parade."

Assad Shoman, in his *Thirteen Chapters of a History of Belize*, quotes J. Eric Thompson who believes that "Cowpen may be an ancient anglicized version of Campin, developed by logwood cutters, just as Sibun and Sittee have come down from Maya Xibun and Zoite" (p. 11).

Curious visitors, as well as serious scholars, are always seeking clues to those thousands of years when Belize and much of the surrounding area was Maya land. The current Maya, while deeply interested in their history, are even more interested in their present and their future. One of them, Ernesto Saqui of Maya Center, Director of the Cockscomb Basin Wildlife Sanctuary in the Stann Creek District, says that the people regard the past with reverence, the future with realism and hope. He urges that movement forward be taken very seriously.

"We need to consider social, religious, and political services, realizing that the work is feasible but difficult. We need to make it vibrant," he says. Speaking of prayer, he reflects, "We like to pray. With guidance we can become independent to do it ourselves."

Ernesto's reference to prayer led to discussion of the churches of many different denominations that had recently found their way down from the States, a situation that had resulted in competition and conflict. Even members of established churches were experiencing pressure to change their membership. He finds the conflict painful; he and many others are looking for ways to overcome it. "We need Ecumenism," he said. "We need to respect other churches and to show that we do."

Ernesto has had a good education, and he wants others to have similar opportunities. He says that the schools in the villages need more music and more sports in their curricula. "People do well," he says, "when given the opportunity." As an example, he tells of the women at the craft center who made $55,000 (Bz.) in three years.

Chico Linares, of Hispanic background but a long time resident of Independence, is enthusiastic about lay ministry. He said, "I feel great about the Church. It has improved since the introduction of lay ministry. Sometimes there are disappointments, but by staying together we are improving."

Chico mentioned development of lay ministry, not only by the sisters, but also by Sharon and Sandy, themselves lay ministers. "It takes all of us," he said. "Otherwise the Church here would have died." He maintains that the Church was dormant when his sons should have been confirmed. Now he finds it difficult to convince them of the value of Confirmation. Chico sees agriculture as Belize's best field of development. He hopes the government will recognize the value of good representation from among the poorer people.

Sharon Cecil, SCNA, has volunteered for Belize twice, for months each time. Here she is cutting grass with a machete—not the way she does it in Kentucky.

"There are problems," he says, "with education." He sees it deteriorating. "Education is actually more costly now, even though the government says that it is free. Books are costly, fees are high." Chico believes that it will change.

Chico's four sons are high school graduates. One of them works with his father, who manages local cable television. One is timekeeper at the banana port. The other two are recent high school graduates.

On the evening of our interview, Chico expressed enthusiasm for the weekly session to plan the coming Sunday liturgy. Soon after reviewing my visit with Chico, I learned that he had had a stroke. At the same time, however, I heard that he is attempting systematically to revive his lost strength. I am told that his sons are spending time with him, helping him to recover. Given his faith and his hopeful approach to life, I am confident that he will make it. He trusts that we are praying for him.

Chico mentioned the lay ministers from the States for whom he has special admiration and appreciation. Sandy Sarangelo Cavolo from Ohio has spent several extended periods in ministry with Paschal and Rosemarie. Sharon Cecil, SCNA, from Kentucky, has likewise volunteered her services twice for several months each time. Sharon says, "Belize touched my life daily. Nowhere in the country did I ever not feel accepted . . . Belize has aroused my innermost feelings for addressing the needs of the poor in that country."

Frequently when SCNs and SCNAs, and others as well, go to Independence, they are impressed by the depth and breadth of relationships that they encounter there. When Marlene Lehmkuhl, SCN, was director of the SCN Associates, she made several trips to Belize in the interest of that program. During one of those visits she and Rosemarie were invited to join a small group of Belizeans for a boat trip on the Caribbean.

They started out in the bright daylight of mid afternoon. Very soon, however, the sky became dark because of sudden stormy weather. Sharing a narrow wooden seat, the two of them held a plastic cover around them, for in the darkness it became very cold. Marlene describes how she was alternating between fear and confidence, when Miss Grace, one of the occupants of the boat, called out, "Look at the moon."

Marlene writes, "I didn't know there was a moon until I turned completely around, the definition of conversion, I know, and became engulfed in the light of the fullest moon. Ahead—dark darkness, behind—luminous light over the vast sea."

Marlene described the Belizean trio—their hosts and hostess. "Ron 'the captain' was about six-foot-four," she states, "handsome in face and physique, in his mid forties, with a head of long dreadlocks, free of inhibitions, 'societal requirements,' disarmingly sensitive, in love with earth, sea, sky, and seafood." Marlene recalls that it was Ron who said, "Come with me around the lagoon." She recalls, too, that midway she had mused, "around the lagoon between Belize and Spain."

"Then," continues Marlene, "there was Pelon-Rafael, the rudder man, a Seventh Day Adventist, knife scars on the right cheek, neck, and arm, imprisoned for fighting while intoxicated, and beaten while imprisoned. Rafael, at the beginning of the sea journey, ventured, 'Let's swap hats.' Ron and Pelon—more synchronized than any keyboard and its computer."

"And finally," concludes Marlene, "Miss Grace, a Canadian, rearing her five children in Norway, widowed, moving to California to be with her children and grandchildren. There she met Ron and came to Belize to build with him their place on the lagoon."

Marlene calls them "three unique but wonderfully close and interdependent persons." She says, "I pondered Grace, calling me out of my fear . . . turning me around to see what was so close, so touchable, so heartening, so empowering . . . ."

In an effort to update accounts like this one of the journey on the lagoon, one must be prepared for both joy and sorrow. Recently I met some of Miss Grace's sorrowing neighbors who told me that soon after the boat ride on the lagoon Miss Grace had become seriously ill. They described Ron's constant, loving care of her, and his painful grief when she died. They had not seen Ron since her death. All development of the place on the lagoon had been left unfinished.

Belize is not extensive if measured in terms of square miles. Anyone who experiences Belize through close association with many of the people, however, finds there immeasurable depth. One tends to locate each group in a particular part of the country. For example, when Orange Walk in the north is mentioned, a predominantly Hispanic people comes to mind, a people whose ancestors came down from Mexico. Many people in Cayo are likewise of Hispanic ancestry and have retained many Hispanic customs. The Cayo and the Orange Walk people reflect different Hispanic characteristics, however, a difference that is difficult to describe, found chiefly in customs. Most people in both places speak English, of course, as do the people of Belize generally.

Dangriga in the Stann Creek District is an important center of Garifuna culture, although, as mentioned in Chapter One, there are Garifuna throughout the land and in many other lands, despite their being only about seven percent of the population of Belize. Theirs is a strong culture. Many of them are teachers. As Barry points out, "In the 1980s there was a surge of cultural identity among the Garifuna, with many communities taking steps to foster pride in their customs and language. As part of this cultural revival, it has been suggested that the term Garinigu—their name for themselves—be put into wider public use" (p. 74).

The Creole people, who are most numerous, are found everywhere in Belize, but Belize City is home to the greatest number. Besides speaking very good English, they speak a basically English patois that has been adopted by most people throughout the country.

The Maya, both the Mopan and the Ketchi, are really the native Belizeans. They are found throughout the country, but are located specifically in certain places. We saw their almost total occupancy of San Antonio, for example. In settlements such as that, the government allows autonomy. The Yuchatachian Maya live chiefly in the north.

Sister Rosemarie Kirwan tells of an experience that reveals a special characteristic of the Maya people, their approach to the sacred. One evening Meme Zabaneh invited Rosemarie and Paschal to go with him and his wife Blanca to Bladen, where his banana farm was located. He had told them of one of the Mayan houses that the people were preparing to use as a church, and of an altar that the people had carved out of wood. That precious wood had lent itself even to the carving of about a dozen pews.

"That was to be the evening of the blessing," says Rosemarie. She asked Meme, "Who is doing the blessing?"

"Well, I suppose you two are," he responded, to her surprise.

Her story continues, "When we got there, it was past dusk. Nowhere to be found was the person who was supposed to have operated the generator, so, of course, there were no lights. Meme took us on a tour of the plantation; in the dark, we appreciated the tour of such places as the packing shed more by faith than by sight."

At that point, the group turned around and saw, according to Rosemarie, a sight that seemed like a mystical experience. Coming from the other side of the road were, perhaps, fifty men, women, and children, many of them carrying either candles or flashlights. The procession moved in silence, as they crossed the road and proceeded down the "roadway" between the houses to the church. There one of the elders, holding a plaster-of-Paris plaque of the Blessed Trinity, stood in front of the doorway. On either side was an older Ketchi woman, each of whom held a thurible made of a powdered milk can from which bellowed plumes of incense. Another elder, who carried a statue of the Sacred Heart, was likewise accompanied by incense-bearing women.

The two men bowed to each other, and then the one with the Sacred Heart statue, with his incense-bearers, thrice circled the would-be church. Bowing in deep reverence at the entrance, they then went into the church, followed by the others and then by as many people as could get in. Since this would be an all-night blessing, children took their places on pieces of plastic in front of the altar.

"After having observed part of the ceremonies through a window," says Rosemarie, "I was invited into the church and given a seat on a stool. Fronds of palm were standing upright along the wall behind the altar, and over the altar was hung a cross made from four fronds. A marimba had been brought in for the occasion. Prayers and exhortations in both Ketchi and Spanish and the playing of the marimba were part of the ceremonies. No book of ritual was used, no priest was present, no holy water was sprinkled. Nevertheless," says Rosemarie, "I felt that the church was truly blessed. The people had proclaimed this spot to be holy ground. Here was an example of lay leadership I had not dreamed of."

Some months later, when the people felt the need of a larger church, Rosemarie was present once more for the blessing. "Although there was attention and respect," she says, "while the official ceremony was being conducted by a priest, the people seemed to be observing a foreign ritual. The ceremony seemed to lack the deep reverence of the first one. How can we learn the sacredness of a culture and realize that God is truly present to the people of God in a variety of ways?" she asks.

Stories abound that reflect the multicultural presence in Belize, and each one is so moving that there is a temptation to tell more and more of them. We say rather, "Visit there, see and hear for yourself, being sure, of course, to drink the water so that you will be assured of returning."

Buildings erected by the Hercules Vegetable Company were given to Independence when the company moved away. They were used as school buildings for many years. When the new school was built and most of the old buildings razed, these two were retained to be used as church (at right) and auditorium.

Meanwhile, it is important to glimpse something of everyday life in Independence. Rosemarie, annalist for that local community, kept an almost daily account of the happenings there. Using those annals in addition to an occasional conversation with Paschal and Rosemarie furnished just the glimpse that we had hoped for.

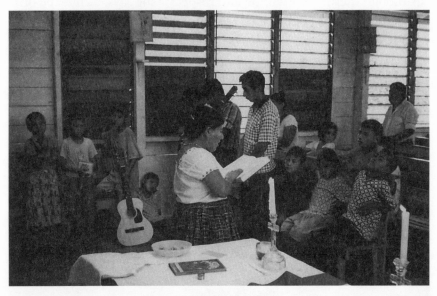

Inside the church, musicians tune up before Mass.

Chapter Eighteen

A New Approach
to the Center

In the early days of the mission at Independence, the SCNs had spent much of their time giving private instruction to young women who were preparing for the examination by means of which they hoped to receive the Graduate Equivalency Diploma. That program, known as GED, had been developed to help mature students, whose high school education had been delayed, to merit the equivalent of a high school certificate. The several young women whom the SCNs assisted were from areas in which there was no access to high school education. Information about those students was conveniently accessible in the annals of the mission, annals well kept by Rosemarie Kirwan, SCN. A few excerpts from later entries, this time the *Annals of 1998*, give further insight into daily life in Independence, life that had become extremely busy and much more demanding than quiet coaching, as important as that had been.

> April 5   After Palm Sunday services here, Rosemarie and Paschal went to Red Bank Village to celebrate with the Indian villages of Santa Rosa, San Roman, San Pablo, and Maya Center. The priest had already been to Seine Bight before reaching Independence; he still had another service at Dangriga.

> April 11   We went to Belize City on the early bus in order to be able to celebrate the Easter Vigil with our visitor, Liz Wendeln, President of our Congregation. There we joined SCN Brenda Gonzales who has been in ministry in Belize City full-

time since last fall, and Higinia Bol of Belize, who told us that she will soon enter the SCN pre-novice program. The president makes regular visits to the houses of the Congregation.

April 14   We went to Hopkins to meet Kitty Wilson and her group of seven young people coming from Northern Mississippi to attend the Youth Jamboree. We visited with them for about an hour.

April 19   We transported the people from old San Juan to Bella Vista for Mass.The people in Bella Vista had not received word about Mass, so only the people from old San Juan were there. In the afternoon Paschal had a meeting with the local lay ministers to prepare them for giving baptismal instruction to the people here. Three of the five were able to come.

April 21   Shortly after seven we heard "Good Morning." Veronica had come again from Punta Gorda for help with her high school studies. She worked until about 1:30 p.m., when we left with her so that she might catch the bus for home. Arriving on that bus were SCNs Kitty Wilson and Theresa Knabel. Theresa had arrived in the country on the nineteenth, her first visit as one participating in a plan to introduce as many SCNs as possible to the country and people of Belize.

April 22   Rosemarie took Kitty and Theresa to Bella Vista, through the banana farms in old San Juan to new San Juan, where they had an opportunity to visit briefly with Carmella Vargas Castillo, SCNA, nurse practitioner for the village. From there we went on to Hopkins to return a photo album to Barbara Nunez, who had coordinated the Youth Jamboree. We had dinner there at the little restaurant, "Over the Waves." Coming home the dust was unbelievable, reducing visibility to about ten feet. There were heavy clouds, producing only about ten raindrops on the windshield but welcome rain came during the night.

April 23   Alarms began going off at 4:45 a.m. Theresa and Kitty were leaving on the six o'clock bus. Paschal had prepared a lovely breakfast for them, including one of her special yeast breads.

After dinner Paschal went to the high school, where she is on the board. She had been called to provide counseling for some students who are in danger of being expelled.

Arriving there, she found that the principal had left without informing her that the session had been postponed. [An oversight such as that, difficult for people of the United States to understand, is not infrequent in Belize. One learns to accept it, while, at the same time, trying diplomatically to have it recognized and changed. In fairness, however, it must be said that such a practice is not universal in Belize. Some Belizeans will not tolerate it.]

After Mathea Bol's tutoring session, Paschal and Rosemarie went on an informational tour: (1) to San Juan to inform the leaders of the union of a meeting to be held at our home on Monday; (2) to several places to give information about travel arrangements for those going to the lay ministers' gathering Thursday; (3) then through the farms to Bella Vista to inform those going from there. [Telephones are not numerous in that area.]

We left on the early bus for Belize City, where we spent the night at the new SCN Center. The next day we obtained our tax releases for use in our upcoming trip to the States. [People leaving Belize are required to present themselves at the tax office, where their records are examined. If they owe taxes, those taxes must be paid before they can leave the country. If they owe none, they are given a tax release form to present with their ticket at departure time.]

April 27   Today things took a surprise turn. Dean Roaches at SPEAR (Society for Progress in Education and Research) asked Paschal to have the leaders of the UBBWU (Banana Workers Union) and those from Maya Center, who are attempting to help them, to meet at our house at 9 a.m. today. Rosemarie left about 7:10 to pick up the Union members in old San Juan and bring them to the house. They arrived about 8:45. About 9:20 Paschal called SPEAR to find out why the leader had not arrived, only to learn that there had been a mistake in the information she had received. Unusual! SPEAR is usually right on target. Finally, those from Maya Center arrived and they met together. Rosemarie took the Union members to their homes about noon.

Fausta Salaam arrived that afternoon for help with her high school correspondence course before she goes on to the Lay Ministry gathering Thursday.

April 29   Veronica Paiz arrived this morning on the early bus. She too will be going to the Lay Ministers Gathering. We will be helping her with her studies today and tomorrow.

April 30   Paschal, Rosemarie, Fausta, Veronica, and Mathea Bol left for the Lay Ministers Gathering that will open this evening in Belize City. We went first to Dangriga, where we joined other ministers, to travel by chartered bus. Nearly all the ministers from this area who are coming for the Gathering will be staying at SCN Center in Belize City.
—End of excerpt from *Annals*—

One descriptive item in the annals at that time concerned the difficulty that had occurred when a strike among workers had been unsuccessful. The Amnesty Program that followed was initiated to bring settlement. During that time the SCN house in Independence served residents of the villages of Bladen, San Pablo, Bella Vista, San Juan, Trio, Cowpen, and Red Bank. The people from those villages who were requesting permanent residency in Belize brought their required documents to have copies made for the Immigration Department. Those were chiefly people who had come from other Central-American countries in recent years. Most of the older residents have had residency for many years.

The pages from the *Annals of Independence* also give evidence of how very busy ministry there had become. Everything that Paschal and Rosemarie were doing was important. After five years of ministry, however, an evaluation of the mission in the fall of 1999 showed that it had reached a point at which it was ready for a new approach. Although it is a mission from Sacred Heart Parish in Dangriga, the church had become like a small parish itself, as had many of the other village churches served from Independence. Likewise, lay ministry programs had been established, with ministers prepared to conduct paraliturgies when it was not the Sunday for the priest to come. A renewed sense of responsibility had developed among the people for attending the liturgies and paraliturgies. There was a general revival of awareness by the people of their responsibility for one another and of their ability to assist one another in many things for which they had become dependent upon the sisters.

In the meantime the SCN congregation, having acquired in Belize City a house now known as SCN Center Belize, saw that ministry could be made stronger and broader by locating all four sisters in the Center, from which some would go out to the many towns and villages.

In July 2000, therefore, Paschal and Rosemarie left Independence, after having planned with the people there and the people of the other villages for a schedule of regular monthly visits. It was understood by the people and by the sisters that those visits would not be only brief friendly calls but also well planned work sessions that the people themselves would be responsible for continuing during the intervening weeks.

SCN Mary Margaret Cooper, better known as Maggie, had joined Brenda Gonzales in Belize City in September 1999. During the year, she had been in ministry in the city with Brenda, as well as in the towns and villages with Paschal and Rosemarie. Maggie's coming not only increased SCN presence in Belize but also made possible the restructuring of the SCN ministry schedule there. The group planned a two-year program directed toward strengthening faith, prayer, and cultural values. In order to assure the latter, they grouped the towns and villages as follows:

HISPANIC—Bella Vista, Cowpen, San Juan, Independence;

MAYA-MOPAN and KETCHI—Maya Center, Maya-Mopan, San Roman, Red Bank, Santa Rosa, San Pablo;

GARIFUNA—Hopkins, Seine Bight, Georgetown.

The first two groups plan to rotate the place of meeting. The third will find it more convenient to meet always in Dangriga, inviting the people there to join in their meetings. The meetings are to consist of prayer, input on such topics as scripture or liturgy, sharing on those or other subjects, cultural enrichment, a plan of action for the ensuing weeks. Included in the latter will be the ministry of evangelization, not only in their own villages but also in outreach to smaller

areas where people have had to move to obtain employment. There
will be special programs for youth and for women, consultant services for Catholic schools, and other outreach as the needs become
clearer. Throughout the program there will be further development
of lay ministry. At the end of two years, those prepared for and willing to assume the responsibility will be commissioned by the Bishop.

The SCN/A mission in Independence had served well in itself. It
had served also as a vantage point from which to reach out to other villages and to involve those villages in service also. Now, Independence
and those other villages had advanced to a point at which they were
being challenged to assume responsibility, with SCN support and regular assistance, for the continuing development of the mission.

*These eight young Mayans, three girls and five boys, have just received the
Sacrament of Confirmation. In Maya-Mopan, according to Maya custom,
the parents bind the heads of the children as soon as they are confirmed,
symbolizing the preservation of the grace of the Sacrament.*

*In this picture, far left is SCN Rosemarie Kirwan, standing next to Most
Reverend Bishop O.P. Martin. At far right is SCN Paschal Maria Fernicola.
Third from the right in the back row is Rev. Anthony Seibert, pastor of
Sacred Heart Parish, Dangriga, of which Maya-Mopan is a mission.*

Chapter Nineteen

JOURNEYS REMEMBERED

"The history of Maya Center is also my history," says Ernesto Saqui, one of sixteen writers and twelve artists who volunteered to produce a volume entitled *Cockscomb Basin Wildlife Sanctuary*. Ernesto continues:

> My ancestors are Maya Mopan who moved from Guatemala to establish the village of San Antonio in the Toledo District of Belize over 100 years ago. The Government of Belize granted them land as an Indian Reservation.

According to Ernesto that was a successful move and "for many years we practiced our sustainable rotating milpa farming system on this land" (p. 25 ff.).

By the 1970s, however, difficulties began to surface. People were beginning to encroach on "the land we thought was reservation land. The available land was no longer enough to feed all the people" (p. 25).

> We appealed to the Government of Belize, which bought 1,000 acres on the east side of the Southern Highway from Donald Hoo for us to use as farmland and 50 acres on the west side of the highway for a village site. We named the new village Maya Center because we wanted to identify ourselves as a Mayan group. (p. 26)

"After 1985," says Ernesto, "Maya Center flourished" (p. 27). He tells how the government built a new school, a football field, wells with pumps, a health clinic, latrines, a community center, and two feeder roads. Finally, he says that since 1993 the village has gotten a water system, electricity, streets, and telephones. It was to that village that the family of Mary Lynn Fields turned when they were seeking a way to sponsor something substantial in memory of her.

After Lynn had left Belize in 1985 to study in Guatemala and later at Boston College, she returned to Nazareth. From there she went to India in the fall of 1986, participating in the community's "East-West Exchange Program."

From 1987 to 1990, Lynn was Director of the SCNAssociates, with an office at Nazareth, Kentucky. In the fall of 1990, after a two-month sabbatical at Casa de Paz in Belize City, she went to Bolivia and then to Peru to study Spanish. In January of 1991, she entered the Central American University in El Salvador, studying there for a year, after which she became a member of the Mobile Pastoral Team of the Jesuit Refugee Services in San Salvador.

Lynn spent Christmas of 1992 with her family in Louisville, Kentucky. Then in January of 1993, en route once more to El Salvador, she stopped over in Belize. There, toward the end of that Christmas season, was held one of those SCN/OP meetings reported periodically in our minutes. This time there were also two Sisters of Mercy. Rarely do those minutes lack at least one high point that tends to lodge in one's memory.

The point that time was high interest in the soon-to-be-opened SCN house in Independence, the subject of the previous two chapters. All of us—SCNs Barbara Flores, Mary Lynn Fields, Irene Locario, and Mary Ransom Burke; Eileen Hannon, OP; Mary Fahey, RSM; Susan Lachapelle, RSM—were very deeply interested. Lynn was especially so. She shared with us her hope of returning to Belize and said that she would love to come to Independence in another year, at the completion of her commitment to El Salvador.

Further discussion resulted in a recommendation that Lynn and I drive down to Independence, to talk with Beth Zabaneh and others in order to get a kind of preview of the mission-to-be. Neither of us needed further encouragement to undertake the journey. We set out very early next morning and reached Dangriga before noon. We stopped there briefly to speak to the Columban priests at Sacred Heart Parish. Observing our truck and recalling the bumpy road to Independence, they insisted on our taking their brand new truck for the rest of the way and picking up ours on the way back. A gift indeed!

Our thoughts and our conversation that day were present and future oriented. My thoughts today, reflecting on that journey, naturally relate it to the one through Mexico in 1982. Then, Lynn, a seasoned yet young missionary, was supplying an orientation for this old neophyte. Now, age differences had evaporated in the atmosphere of shared experience, and we were both peering into the future with hope and enthusiasm.

Like special recordings in minutes, some events that take place on journeys maintain special niches in one's memory. Two events of the journey hold that kind of place in mine.

As we drove down the highway, we began to see evidence that schools were beginning to dismiss the children from the lower classes. We stopped several times as people began to recognize Lynn and to call to her. One woman begged her to "Wait until my little girl gets home from school. She's your godchild and she's named for you." That picture of those large groups of people, mostly mothers, looking up at Lynn with love and appreciation, has a permanent place in my memory.

When we reached Independence, we went immediately to see Beth Zabaneh about rooms in their motel. There was only one vacant, a single room with a double bed. We took it, grateful that we were no later, for that one would soon have been gone. Weary as we were after our long journey with many stops along the way, we talked far into the night.

Of particular interest to Lynn at that time was a magazine that she shared with me. It was a copy of DISCOVERY: *Jesuit International Ministries*. She was so eager to have me read that new publication that she insisted on my taking it with me. I did take it, intending to return it to her at my earliest opportunity. I still have the magazine. It must have been distributed six months before publication date to a select group of recipients. It is dated May 1993. The accident that took Lynn's life occurred February 12 of that year, just a few weeks after our journey to check out places that we might suggest as appropriate for establishing our mission in Independence.

It is easy to understand why that magazine appealed to Lynn. Featured are two articles by Francisco Claver, SJ, Bishop of Malaybalay in the Philippines and responses from fellow Jesuits in Kenya, Nigeria/Ghana, Sudan, Lebanon, Micronesia, India, Peru, El Salvador, and the United States. In an introduction to the articles, the editor Joseph P. Daoust, SJ, states: "[The Bishop] addresses the need of young churches abroad to move beyond simply receiving from First World churches in the older paradigm of the 'haves' distributing their largesse to the 'have nots.'" Daoust adds, "I think it is just as important for us and for our people to receive from the new young churches. They have the Good News of Christ becoming incarnate in new and marvelous ways in their midst" (p. x).

Between our January journey in Belize and February 12, after I had returned to Nazareth, I had one conversation with Lynn by phone. She called to say that the program to which she had been committed in El Salvador would be terminating in the spring and that she would then be available for Independence, if the community wanted her to go there. She had tried to reach Susan Gatz, our Regional, but had been informed that she was out of town. She asked me to convey to Susan that message.

It was during the morning rush hour of Saturday, February 12, that Lynn was taking two Sisters of Mercy to the airport in San Salvador, when a speeding car crowded her off the road and went speeding on. One of her passengers was slightly injured, the other not at all. Lynn herself was fatally injured. Word of her death reached Nazareth around noon. I remember the effort to reach her mother immediately.

Lynn was waked, and prayer services and the Liturgy of Christian Burial held for her in El Salvador. Her sisters, sisters of other communities, as well as many of her other friends in Belize, went to El Salvador for those services. A number also accompanied her body to Kentucky. There a prayer service was held in the drawing room of the Nazareth Motherhouse Friday evening. After the Mass of Christian Burial, offered Saturday morning in the Cathedral at Bardstown, Lynn was laid to rest in the Nazareth Cemetery.

Lynn's death was a great loss to the Sisters of Charity and to the Fields family—her mother and her six sisters and three brothers. The family wanted to establish in her memory something that would insure that her ministry continue. They set up immediately a corporation, **The Sister Mary Lynn Fields Memorial Fund**, calling it for purposes of easy communication *Lynn's Heart*, with themselves—Catherine Fields, Patricia Wente, Paula Cesler, Karen Johnson, Mike Fields, Jane Fields, Pamela Johnson, Chuck Fields, Tina Beavin, and Joe Fields—as board of directors. The organization's newsletter is also called *Lynn's Heart*.

Their first efforts were directed toward finding a person who would understand the ministry and be willing to carry it on, and toward raising the funds needed to support such an individual. Within little more than two years they found the person, Hermelindo Saqui, a thirty-four-year-old Mayan, brother of Ernesto, who was willing to resign his position with the Audubon Society in order to pursue his own dream, to work with his people in the Stann Creek District of Belize.

In the second issue of their annual brochure they describe Hermelindo as a trained village health worker and lay minister who has chosen to use his talents to fight the social erosion of the Maya people. They quote him as saying, "I have witnessed the destruction of our cultural heritage and customs."

They explain that Hermelindo had for a long time wanted to do that kind of work, but "his hopes and ideals could not bring home food to his wife, Alberta Pop Saqui, or provide clothes for their two beautiful daughters, Mary, eight, and Luchia, seven." "Thanks to the contributors," states the brochure, "that has changed. With a salary made possible by your generous gifts . . . Saqui is now working to change the devastation wrought by decades of cultural and economic oppression."

Saqui says, "Our culture, customs, and beliefs are very important to us. This is what really the late Sister Mary Lynn was teaching us. This is why I, Hermelindo Saqui, truly accept and dedicate myself to continue the good work in the years to come."

Saqui has been a leader in the Mayan protest of the attempted mass clearing of the Maya-Mopan territory by a foreign company and in the effort to have it stopped. The government of Belize, always in need of funds, is approached frequently by such companies that would like to have Belize's valuable wood. Much to Belize's loss, some of those companies have been successful. Increasing awareness on the part of the people, such as the Saquis, however, has resulted in attempts to meet the problem head-on at both national and local levels of government. Evidently the Fields' choice of Hermelindo was truly wise.

Hermelindo Saqui with SCN Kitty Wilson. Kitty has been a part of the SCN Belize story from the late seventies to the present. Besides spending four years in ministry in the beginning, she has conducted tours in Belize for people from the States. She has spent months in Belize making valuable studies. The results of some of the studies have had extensive classroom use.

Little by little the non-profit foundation of the Fields family, which donates time and subsidizes costs, has been able to contribute more than the on-going salary and running expenses for Hermelindo. For example, a group calling themselves Buenos Amigos, refugees from other Central-American countries who had come to peaceful Belize for safety and freedom, had run into difficulty with the government. As a result they had set up a kind of cooperative among themselves. Assisted and encouraged by Marciana Funes, leader of those who had participated in a strike, they started a large farm on land that belonged to the Funes family. The farm itself was proving successful, but they were in need of a truck to take the vegetables to market. Otherwise all would be lost. Once again *Lynn's Heart* came to the rescue. A truck was located and purchased for $10,000.

The next project was the purchase of a portable generator to assist Hermelindo with his work in the villages. That was the year, 1998, when the family foundation made a donation also to Sacred Heart Parish in Dangriga, "which educates 3,000 students a year, provides assistance to thousands of families, and employs more than 100 people."

Brochure #5 features a column and a half entitled "The Future." The following is part of that story:

> Now entering our fifth year, *Lynn's Heart* continues to plot its course, looking for ways to make the most significant and meaningful impact on the lives of the disadvantaged in the back country of Belize.

The family meets periodically as the Board of Trustees of the **Sister Mary Lynn Fields Memorial Fund**. They review the report of Hermelindo Saqui, evaluate the results of the other on-going projects, and plan for the future.

The previous sentence would have brought this chapter to a close, had not a devastating hurricane struck Belize October 7, 2001. Other comparable occurrences in 1931 and 1961, as well as lesser ones in subsequent years, had been accepted in a trustful spirit. The hurricane, while not causing great loss of life like the earlier ones, wrought widespread destruction. For example, it destroyed nearly all the Maya homes as well as the palm trees needed to reconstruct them. It wiped out the current banana crop; it destroyed nearly a dozen schools. Large-scale financial assistance was needed to rebuild and replant. The Red Cross moved in immediately. Many church-related groups as well as others who are aware of the needs are assisting in many ways. For example, the Fields family helped the Church directly in its many rebuilding efforts and supported Hermelindo in the difficult task of finding and assisting people in remote areas.

SCNs Maggie Cooper and Rosemarie Kirwan, instead of holding classes in the Stann Creek District as usual, visited there to deliver food and supplies. Caritas Lawrence, RSM, recently returned to Belize after having lived for four years with SCNs in Louisville while attending Spalding University, directed truckloads of supplies to the stricken districts. An undetermined amount of time and money will be required to restore the stricken parts of Belize to normalcy.

Fortunately, however, the construction of the church at Maya Center was not seriously hampered by the hurricane. In fact, it has been completed and was dedicated early in 2002. Knowing Belizeans, and trusting in the help of their many friends, no one doubts the country's complete recovery. Belize will make it; it always does.

Chapter Twenty

MILLENNIAL SPRINGBOARD: SCN CENTER BELIZE

As the twentieth century was racing toward its close, and prophets of doom were predicting a dire future, if any, SCNs, Associates, and friends were planning to celebrate the twenty-fifth anniversary of the Congregation's presence in Belize. Leading up to that celebration there had been several years' effort to enable the mission to become better focused. All SCNs and those who had ministered with them through the years had hoped, in the interest of stability, that the Congregation might some day establish a central house in Belize rather than depend entirely on whatever housing might be available at the scene of each mission.

As in most countries, in order to own property in Belize it is necessary to become a corporation within that country. That legal procedure was followed and a house acquired by 1997. Located on Princess Margaret Drive across from a large fishery and with a sweeping view of the Caribbean, SCN Center Belize promises to be a firm SCN/A springboard to the future.

The Center was blessed September 27, feast of St. Vincent de Paul, 1998. As Bishop Martin moved throughout the building, blessing its smallest pantry as well as the broad open porches, the large group moving with him sang Christopher Beatty's "This is holy ground; you are standing on holy ground, for God is present, and where God is is holy."

Observing that group was like a memory trip through the years. There were people from every walk of life—lay ministers, associates, sisters of several communities, priests and brothers, men and women from several parishes, all singing of holy ground. It was evident that not only were the grounds and the building receiving a very special blessing, but also our mission was being blessed by those people whose friendship had blessed us for many years and whose presence that day gave us courage to continue to walk with them in ministry.

As solemn as the blessing was, Bishop Martin's humorous comments, as he moved from top floor to ground floor, lightened the atmosphere on that Sunday afternoon when the thermometer was registering higher and higher. At the close of the ceremony, the participants welcomed cool refreshments while they enjoyed conversations that combined memories and talk of the future.

SCN Brenda Gonzales, who hosted the reception that followed the blessing, was assisted by Higinia Bol, teacher in Holy Redeemer School and resident at the Center, and by SCNs Paschal Maria Fernicola and Rosemarie Kirwan from Independence. Higinia would soon be moving to the Novitiate of the Congregation at Nazareth, Kentucky. Brenda would continue to "hold the fort" until SCN Mary Margaret Cooper would join her in the fall of 1999. Then Paschal and Rosemarie would leave their residence in Independence to complete the community at the Center in Belize City in July of 2000.

Even before Brenda's local community increased to two and then to four, however, she was seldom alone. Long before taking up residence in Belize, while she was still a member of the faculty of Loyola University in Chicago, Brenda was conducting programs in in-service learning that brought students to Belize during breaks in their academic schedules. In varying periods of time, students had an opportunity to become well acquainted with a culture other than their own. The great number of students at Loyola and other universities asking to be included in the alternative break program led Brenda and the Executive Committee of the Congregation to see the value of Brenda's moving to Belize in order to be on hand to prepare for and receive the groups rather than to accompany them to Belize from the States.

A brochure that describes the combined Immersion and Service Experience explains:

> At the center volunteers will receive orientation to Belize and its diverse cultures prior to being placed in such service areas as the Mercy Health Clinic and the Child Development Center. The volunteers will have a chance to experience the foods, the visual arts, the music, the pace of life in Belize. Opportunities for prayer and reflection together, and with Belizeans, will provide the visiting youth support and guidance as they seek the deeper meaning of their experiences.

That announcement was hardly off the press when the Center was flooded with applications for participation. As Brenda commented, "This surprising response confirmed the need for such a program."

The three-story building had not been completely renovated to accommodate groups, but those first applicants were accepted and they actually helped to make the final adjustments. The local community of SCNs is housed on the top floor. The first and second floors have dormitories that house eighteen persons with an additional five private bedrooms, kitchens, laundry, four bathrooms, dining room, chapel, several large areas for group gatherings, a veranda, and a large yard. The garage has been converted into a dormitory. For three years the place has been serving well the needs of the programs.

In addition to both formal and informal evaluation, free flowing comments from participants themselves attest to the value of the program. Carol Villafane, for example, a senior at Loyola University and a student coordinator for HCOE (Hispanic Center of Excellence) at the College of Medicine at the University of Chicago, writes in *¡Adelante!* Fall/Winter, 1999: "This past May I had the opportunity to do volunteer work in Belize City, Belize. The week I spent with those children was one of the best experiences of my life. I arrived in Belize thinking I was going to teach children some simple ABCs; instead, they taught me a few lessons about my life."

Carol explains that both she and the children walked about thirty minutes to school from different localities in ninety-degree weather. When she arrived each morning she was greeted with hugs and a "Good morning, teacher Carol." She describes the poverty of books and supplies, in the midst of which she says, "I had never met such an energetic and physically resilient group of four-year-olds in my life."

Carol says, "Throughout my trip, I marveled that no matter how poor or disadvantaged the people I met were, they were never unhappy . . . . This trip strengthened my motivation to become a doctor and to practice in underserved areas, whether in Chicago or Latin America."

The *Lexington Herald-Leader*, August 5, 1998, carried a lead article, subtitled "Service Trip to Belize, a stirring experience for Lexington teens." The opening paragraph quotes Nicola Jennings, a recent graduate of Lexington Catholic High School in Lexington, Kentucky, as saying, "I couldn't imagine going to the stores and buying all this stuff when down there they don't even have diapers." Nicola was explaining why she couldn't go on a family shopping tour the day she returned from Belize.

Amina Bejos, SCN, a member of the Religion Department of that high school, and herself a Belizean, said, "I wanted to give these students the opportunity to experience other cultures, especially cultures where people may not have much, but they are still incredibly happy."

Evan Fugassi, another of those students, said, "I think the most we took away from it was the experience with the people. Sure, we got to see the country, but I can remember more easily a woman I met than I do the Mayan ruins. When the first thing that comes to your mind is a person, you know it's more than just a vacation." These comments are typical of students who take part in one or more of the programs.

In talking about those students, Brenda mentioned more than twenty schools and universities from which they come. Among those institutions were the following: Loyola University and Loyola

University Medical College in Chicago; Boston College; Rush University; Seattle University; Virginia Commonwealth University; Spalding University, Louisville, Kentucky; and Peaceworks.

Meanwhile, schools and special programs in Belize have not been overlooked. Among the twenty or more that Brenda mentioned were the following: the Jesuit International Volunteers, Habitat for Humanity International, the Sisters of Mercy and their Associates at the Kitchen, Clinic, and Sister Cecilia Home; HelpAge for the Elderly; Stella Maris, a Special Education Unit for Belize Schools; Catholic Diocesan Child Development Center; St. Martin's Parish School; St. John's College; and Lay Ministers for the Diocese.

As we reviewed this broad network, Brenda reminded me that in this, and throughout her ministry, she bases her plans on the SCN Mission Statement:

> We Sisters of Charity of Nazareth are an international congregation in a multicultural world. Impelled by the love of Christ, in the tradition of Vincent de Paul and the pioneer spirit of Catherine Spalding, we and our Associates are committed to work for justice in solidarity with oppressed peoples, especially the economically poor and women; and to care for the earth. We risk our lives and resources, both personally and corporately, as we engage in diverse ministries in carrying out this mission.

This Mission Statement is, of course, the foundation of SCN ministry in the Stann Creek District as described in Chapter Ten. Sisters Brenda, Paschal, Rosemarie, and Maggie share ministry in Belize City and Stann Creek District. As they meet the many people with whom and for whom they minister, stretching as far as four strong, zealous women can reach, they hope and pray for others to join them. They need those others both now and in the future. The call is to join them, not only in Belize City and the Stann Creek District, but also in the Cayo and Toledo districts described in earlier chapters. The needs summarized in Chapter Eight are so numerous and so varied as to challenge a host of women and men, lay and religious,

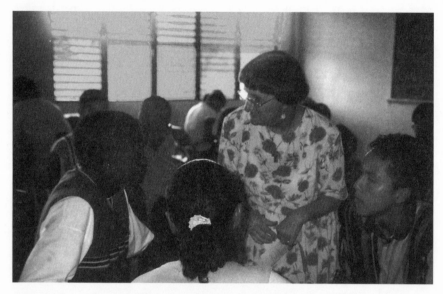

SCN Maggie Cooper is teaching a class in Religion at St. John's College.

to respond to that call, a call that comes from the heart of Christ for the people of Belize.

As we go to press, 2003, Maggie Cooper, SCN, is teaching a class in religion at St. John's College. She has arranged with Loyola University in New Orleans for students to complete the full degree. Joining her in this endeavor are Barbara Flores, SCN, and several Jesuits on the faculty at St. John's. The response of nearly twice the number expected seeking admission more than proved the need.

While we look to the future and always hope for "new recruits," we continue to celebrate the past upon which the new is built. Because Dangriga was the SCN starting place in Belize, Sacred Heart Church there was the place chosen for the Silver Jubilee Celebration. The Mass of Thanksgiving, offered there Sunday, September 3, 2000, was concelebrated by His Excellency Osmond P. Martin, Bishop of Belize City and Belmopan, and His Excellency Kendrick Williams, Bishop of Lexington, Kentucky. An account of Bishop Williams's relationship to SCN history in Belize and of his place in the development of ministry in Belize generally is found in Chapter Three.

In his homily, Bishop Martin reiterated the welcome expressed before the liturgy by Barbara Flores, SCN, to more than five hundred priests, religious, and laity, who had come from throughout the country, as well as from the United States, to participate in the celebration. The Bishop expressed gratitude for the presence and the service of the Sisters and of their Associates. He recalled his visit to the Motherhouse at Nazareth, Kentucky, during a General Assembly a decade earlier. He even quoted from an address by Dorothy Mac-Dougall, SCN, President of the Congregation at that time. Fortunately, Dorothy was present in Dangriga that day for the celebration.

Representing the current president was Mary Elizabeth Miller, SCN, Vice President, who voiced the Congregation's happiness at the privilege of serving in Belize. She expressed the regrets of President Maria Vincent Brocato, SCN, who was recovering from an injury. The liturgy, characterized by traditional Garifuna movement and by Mestizo and Maya hymns, was followed by dinner and a cultural program in the church-school compound.

John Canoe, whom we met in Chapter Two, entertains the many people celebrating the anniversary. The people are seated at tables on the long porch of the school or on the steps leading to the porch.

Maya-Mopan and Ketchi dancers join John Canoe in celebrating the jubilee.

At the close of that celebration in Dangriga, some SCNs, Associates, and friends remained to visit with old friends and to have an SCNA meeting. Others set off to visit places that had been sites of early ministry. There were representatives of the people from those places at the Dangriga celebration, but the real reunions took place when SCNs went to San Ignacio, Independence, San Antonio, and many other places along the way. While reminiscing and "catching up," participants shared glimpses of the future and expressions of hope.

At the SCNA meeting in Dangriga, in addition to the joy of renewing old friendships and meeting new members, conversation was dotted with "remember when," for it was in Dangriga that the Belizean SCNAssociate Program was established. In 1976 Lynn had invited SCN Carol Clasgens to come with a group of students from Memphis Catholic High to introduce the Search retreat. Then a group of Belizean students had gone to Memphis to see it in operation there (see Chapter 5). Some of the Belizean students later became SCNAs. That exchange of past and current experiences might have extended endlessly had not someone asked Carmella Vargas Castillo about her recent experience at the United Nations.

Shalini D'Souza, SCN Vice President, nominated Carmella to membership on the Forum, and the Congregation sponsored her attendance, May 20-26, 2000. Carmella was one of three persons selected to represent the Sisters of Charity Federation. The other two were Eva Boyle Bianchi from Peru and Maria Eugenia Romero de Tello from Ecuador. The week-long meeting utilized all the facilities of the UN, such as instant translation. The purpose of the meeting, according to Carmella, was (1) to give the people of the very poor nations as true a picture as possible of world economy; (2) to educate the grassroots about the whole idea of Globalization and the need for recognition of everybody at every level. Carmella quoted one speaker as saying, "Somebody needs to take up the challenge to educate the people at the lower level."

Carmella Vargas Castillo, SCNA, who spoke at the Peoples' Millenium Forum of the UN-NGO Meeting in May 2000 as a Representative of the Sisters of Charity Federation, is pictured with other Federation Representatives: left to right, Eva Boyle Bianchi, Peru, Carmella Vargas Castillo, SCNA, Belize, Maria Eugenia Romero de Tello, Ecuador, and Barbara Padilla, SC, Cincinnati, Ohio.

Carmella explained that there was a large forum every day at which members were encouraged to express opinions. Then followed smaller group sessions where certain aspects of the forum were discussed. She called those sessions meetings for fine-tuning. She attended those on "Human Rights," "Eradication of Poverty," and "Challenges of Globalization."

The forum centered, she said, on indigenous people and their interests. Carmella discussed the concerns of the Maya and the Garifuna. She included education, health care, and lack of facilities in many departments. She stressed the necessity of preserving each culture and of maintaining the identity of each. She spoke of the poor wages paid by outside agencies, especially in the banana industry, and about the poor working conditions in that area. She stressed the greed for profit and the need for employers to enter into collaboration with employees. The forum placed great emphasis on teaching about human rights in schools. One recurring theme was the necessity for the superpowers to put the same amount of money into education for peace as they put into nuclear testing.

When I had an opportunity to speak with Carmella later, she mentioned the insistence on three words: conscientization, liberation, capacitation. The first, she said, refers to the obligation of heads of governments to let the voices of the voiceless be heard. The second refers to insistence on the education of workers. The third is defined as the empowerment of the poor and less fortunate to speak for their rights.

Broad discussion had covered the failure on the part of the poor to speak out for their rights for fear of losing their jobs, of being abused, deported, or killed. Speakers emphasized the need for grassroots people to organize themselves to support their cause. One slogan was: "There is power and strength where there is unity." Insistence on restoring the integrity of the family was paramount.

Delegates agreed that if the UN and the Human Rights Commission ignore the problems considered in the conference, deadly problems will continue throughout the world, problems such as

AIDS, dysfunctional families, general family breakdown. Leaders urged participants, upon return to their countries, to hold workshops on Human Rights, to identify people with good leadership skills, and to pay their salaries to work as human rights advocates in those countries. Reminders about the costs and dangers attached to the work were also given.

As an afterthought, Carmella recalled the thin line between war and peace that was evident among the Israelis and the Palestinians attending the meeting. Carmella's gifts and her courage to speak out were evidently recognized at the conference. She continued to speak out when she returned home. Maggie, Paschal, and Rosemarie have remarked on how very good her reports were and have noted that each time she spoke the people gave her a standing ovation.

As I reflect on Carmella's experience, I find myself admiring the effort of the United Nations to enlighten the people of the poorer nations. At the same time I wonder how Carmella and others like her will be able to raise the necessary funds to support leaders to work as human rights advocates. We need to encourage Carmella and her counterparts in the other poor nations to try to put into effect all that they learned at the UN in May 2000. Is that all we can do?

I don't know the answer to that question. I simply present the picture as it has been presented to me, and I hope that those who do know the answer will share it with conviction—conviction leading to action.

AFTERWORD

Although the Sisters of Charity cannot answer the question raised at the end of Chapter Twenty, they can and are attempting to comment on the plans for the future of SCN Belize. As the Congregation began the development of a revised government structure in the new millennium, special attention was directed to those missions outside of either India or the United States. Belize is one of those missions.

In this latest move, the SCN mission in Belize becomes directly responsible to the Central Government of the Congregation in the person of the Vice President, currently Shalini D'Souza. Since the beginning of the mission in 1975, Belize had been a part of that area most recently called the Southern Region.

The recent decision of the Congregation to reorganize its government structure has led to a detailed study of each part. One phase was a careful self-study by the six SCNs in mission at SCN Center Belize at that time, facilitated by Shalini and Maria Rieckelman, MM. Beginning the evening of September 12 and continuing through September 18, 2002, the mission was studied in detail.

Participating in the analysis was the current SCN local community of SCN Center Belize: Barbara Flores, Higinia Bol, Mary Margaret Cooper, Rosemarie Kirwan, Teresa Rose Nabholz, and Beverly Hoffman, who is currently considering the possibility of becoming a member of the local community.

High points of the seven-day study included the possibility of expanding the mission and new ways of being in ministry in Belize. Included in the new ways is a residential program for young women seriously considering membership in the community. The purpose, of course, is to encourage authentic indigenous vocations and associate membership.

Consideration of "new ways" concentrated on the value of relationship with Central Government rather than being attached to a province close by in matter of miles but of a culture differing from the indigenous culture of Belize. Maria Rieckelman stressed the need for *sturdiness* and awareness of the value of an authentic counterculture.

As an observer of SCN ministry in Belize for twenty-seven years and as a participant in the mission there for six of those years plus two extended research visits, I am ready to close this book on a note of gratitude. Life has taught me, however, not to sound that note with too much volume until the plans are carried out. I am confident the next narrator will recount the happy outcome. Similar plans have been attempted previously, but none with the thoroughness of this one.

I am moved to close with the last lines of the poem from Chapter 14:

> but still it seems there's something else,
> something about to happen,
> as if sometime when I look down to avoid a pool
> left by last night's rain,
> I'll look up suddenly and see
> that sparkle of the sun upon the sea
> has washed over the land,
> removing the layer of roughness
> and leaving only the beauty that is really there.

TIME LINE

1974   The Church in Belize requests Sisters of Charity of Nazareth to minister in Dangriga. Two SCNs—Mary Lynn Fields and Susan Gatz—spend the summer investigating the mission.

1975   The *Justice '75* program brings SCN presence to Belize. SCN Kitty Wilson begins ministry in San Antonio as part of that program.

Liz Wendeln, SCN, and Father Ken Williams conduct, at Nazareth, a team planning workshop for ministry in Belize.

Mary Lynn Fields returns to Dangriga where she is joined by Marian Joseph Baird, RSM, in a house provided for them by the parish.

1976   Workshops are presented in Stann Creek and Cayo Districts by the team from Kentucky. Lay Ministry Program develops in the Stann Creek District.

SCN Carol Clasgens and a group of students from Memphis Catholic High introduce the "Search" retreat in Dangriga.

Anna Marie Nalley, SCN, begins nursing ministry in Belize.

Kitty Wilson returns to Belize to minister in Dangriga. Judy Raley, SCN, begins pastoral ministry in Dangriga.

1977   The January issue of the *Catholic Bulletin* lists a pastoral team of seven in Dangriga and announces the first meeting for the Ministers of the Word Program to be held January 15 and 16.

1978   In January, the first group of lay ministers for Stann Creek District is commissioned by Bishop Robert L. Hodapp.

SCNs Judy Raley and Kitty Wilson, two Pallottine sisters, and two priests form a ministry team in San Ignacio.

1980   Kitty returns to the States.

1981   Belize becomes independent on September 21. The old problem of the Guatemalan claim is revived.

SCN Sarah Ferriell succeeds Lynn Fields in the SCN mission in Dangriga.

SCN Barbara Flores begins pastoral ministry in Dangriga.

1982   In January, SCNs Lynn Fields and Mary Ransom Burke open a mission in Belize City. SCNs minister full time in Toledo District.

The first commissioning in the Toledo District took place on February 14.

1983   The first group of lay ministers for Belize City is commissioned by Bishop Hodapp in Holy Redeemer Cathedral on January 23.

On March 9, Pope John Paul II visits Belize.

Ann Moyalan, SCN, from India begins working with Anna Marie Nalley in San Antonio. She is joined by SCN John Loretto Mueller, who is to work with the parish team and the teachers. In a few months, Ann succeeds Anna Marie as director of nursing in San Antonio after the latter's illness.

1984   Judy Raley returns to Nazareth to become Secretary General of the SCN Congregation. SCN Ann Kernen takes over the ministry in San Ignacio.

Barbara Flores leaves for the States to study at Spalding University.

The first National Gathering of Lay Ministers is held in San Ignacio, March 9–11.

Women religious of Belize City plan to establish a Child Development Center.

1985   In January, Irene Locario, recently professed as a Sister of Charity of Nazareth, arrives in San Antonio to teach full time in the school.

Adeline Fehribach, SCN, begins pastoral ministry in Dangriga.

Lynn Fields leaves Belize to study in Guatemala and later at Boston College.

Elizabeth Miles, OP, joins Ransom in Belize City.

1986 The regional representative of St. Vincent de Paul Society comes to establish officially a branch of the Society in the country of Belize.

Columban Fathers from Ireland, at the invitation of Bishop Osmond P. Martin, begin to fill vacancies in some Belizean parishes.

The Lay Ministry Program directed by SCNs Jane Karakunnel from India and John Loretto Mueller is still strong in San Antonio.

John Loretto takes fifty-nine catechists to Belize City for the National Gathering.

Mary Otho Ballard, OP; SCNs Jane Karakunnel and Amina Bejos; and Higinia Bol conduct Bible School in Crique Sarco, remote village in the Toledo District.

Jane returns to San Antonio, where she and John Loretto prepare candidates for commissioning as catechists.

A census in Yarborough gives evidence of the need for a school in that area of Belize City.

SCN/OP meeting is held in Guatemala in September to review and evaluate ministry in Belize; present are the Regional and the SCNs from Dangriga, San Antonio, San Ignacio, and Belize City.

SCN Amina Bejos becomes Director of Catechetics in Dangriga.

Sarah Ferriell leaves Dangriga to return to the States.

1987 SCNs in Belize celebrate 175 years since the founding of the Congregation in Kentucky.

Irene Locario leaves Belize to study at Spalding University.

Barbara Flores returns to Belize as Director of the Diocesan Catechetical Program.

SCN Paschal Maria Fernicola joins Ann Kernen in San Ignacio.

After five years in Belize City, Ransom returns to Nazareth, Kentucky.

1988   Elizabeth Miles is elected general of her Dominican congregation and returns to the Motherhouse in Kentucky.

SCNs Barbara Flores and Irene Locario remain at the SCN house in the City. Barbara is Diocesan Director of Religious Education for the Catholic Schools, and Irene is a teacher at St. Martin's School. They are joined by SCNs Jean Kulangara and Ann Kernen, by Dominicans Eileen Hannon and Claire McGowan, RSM Mary Hartnett, and Dominican Sister of the Sick Poor Cecilia Crittenden, all six of whom are in separate ministries.

The school in the Yarborough area of Belize is dedicated.

Elaine McCarron, SCN, spends a three-month sabbatical assisting teachers of religion in Belize.

The Child Development Center opens.

Jane Karakunnel leaves San Antonio to resume her studies in Chicago.

1989   Amina Bejos, Local Manager of Schools (Superintendent) in Stann Creek District, is joined in Dangriga by Ransom and Jean Turney, Jesuit International Volunteer.

Adeline Fehribach returns to the States.

1990   Mary Otho Ballard, OP, who has spent some shorter periods of time in Belize, now comes to San Antonio full-time. She is joined by Paschal Maria Fernicola, who has been in ministry in several places in the country.

Irene Locario begins ministry at St. Martin de Porres School in Belize City.

At a special Belize meeting, called the Belize Party, held during the SCN Assembly, forty-nine people sign a paper, offering to do specific things for Belize.

John Loretto Mueller and Ann Kernen return to Kentucky after six years in San Antonio.

Jean Kulangara leaves Belize to resume her studies at Spalding University.

Amina Bejos returns to the States to study at Spalding University.

1991 Mary Ransom co-chairs with Barbara Flores a movement called the Belize Connection, working separately for a year, after which Ransom goes to Belize to plan with knowledgeable people there.

Kitty Wilson spends six months in Belize writing an instructional text for Confirmation.

1993 Mary Otho returns to Kentucky.

Lynn and Ransom make an overnight trip to Independence to investigate the best place for the SCN house soon to be established.

On February 12, Lynn dies in an automobile accident in El Salvador. The Mass of Christian Burial is celebrated there. Her body is transported to Nazareth. After Mass in the Cathedral in Bardstown, her body is laid to rest in the Nazareth Cemetery.

Paschal Maria Fernicola opens a mission in Independence in the fall. Bishop Martin makes available a house for Paschal and volunteer Clara Cuellar.

The Graduate Equivalency Program (GED) is established for young women.

Clara is replaced by Sandy Sarangelo, volunteer from Ohio, and later by SCN Rosemarie Kirwan in January 1995.

Barbara Flores leaves Belize to study at Boston College.

1995 Irene Locario leaves Belize to study at Spalding University for a year.

1996 Irene begins teaching at St. Catherine Academy in Belize City.

1997 Ransom Burke, SCN, visits Belize to update information and complete research for *We Drank the Water*.

SCN Brenda Gonzales begins an important ministry in Belize. For many years she had been conducting student tours of Belize for college students from the States. Now she hosts those tours in Belize City.

1998   SCNs working with SPEAR (Society for Progress in Education and Research) focus at this time on banana workers and their needs.

The Lay Ministers Gathering is held in Belize.

The house acquired by the Community in Belize City in 1997 becomes SCN Center Belize; blessing occurs September 27.

1999   SCN Mary Margaret Cooper joins Brenda Gonzales in Belize City, working part time with Paschal Maria Fernicola and Rosemarie Kirwan in Stann Creek District.

2000   SCN Congregation makes a decision to have all four sisters live in Belize City, participate in ministry there, going out to the Stann Creek District on selected weekends.

SCNs Celebrate Twenty-five Years of Ministry in Belize.

2001   Paschal Maria Fernicola is recalled to the States because of the serious illness of her mother.

2002   Brenda Gonzales accepts a position in Washington, D.C. as assistant director of the Jesuit Volunteer Program.

SCN Teresa Rose Nabholz begins retreat ministry in Belize City.

SCNs Higinia Bol and Beverly Hoffman join the local community in Belize City.

WORKS CITED

Annals of Sisters of Charity of Nazareth, Independence. Apr. 1998.

Annals of Sisters of Charity of Nazareth, San Antonio. Feb. 1987. July, 1993.

Barry, Tom. *Inside Belize.* Albuquerque: The Inter-Hemispheric Education Resource Center, 1992.

Belize Sunday Times. [Belize City] 27 Sept. 1981.

Belizean Studies I.6. (1978).

The Benedictine Presence in Belize. Benque Viejo: BRC Printing, 1996.

"Bible School at Crique Sarco." *SCNews.* Sept. 1986: 6.

Buhler, Richard, SJ. *A History of the Catholic Church in Belize.* Belize City: BISRA, 1976.

Catholic Bulletin [Belize City] Jan. 9, 1997.

Cayetano, E. Roy. Coordinator and Editor. *People's Garifuna Dictionary.* Belmopan: National Garifuna Council of Belize, 1993.

"Child Development Center Opens." *Christian Herald* [Belize City] Jan. 1989: 1.

Christian Herald [Belize City] Nov. 1979. Oct. 1981.

Daoust, Joseph P., SJ. Introduction. *DISCOVERY: Jesuit International Ministries.* May (1993) x.

Dobson, Narda. *A History of Belize.* Trinidad and Jamaica: Longman Caribbean Limited, 1973 (Rpt. 1979).

Economist [London], quoted in Charles T. Hunter, "The Young Belizean Church...." p. 12. See below.

"Ecumenism, Unity touted in Belize." *National Catholic Reporter* [Kansas City, MO] 18 Mar. 1983: 27.

Edgell, Zee. *Beka Lamb*. Portsmouth, NH: Heinemann, 1982 (1988).

"First Madrecita Convent Opened in Orange Walk Dist. Ceremonies." *Christian Herald* [Belize City] 18 Nov. 1979: 1+.

Gomez, Loraine. "New Executive Committee and Board of Directors for Lay Ministers." *Christian Herald* [Belize City] Oct. 1997.

Gutierrez, Gustavo. *A Theology of Liberation: History, Politics, and Salvation*. Maryknoll, NY: Orbis Books, 1988.

Horizon 2000. Belize City: Angelus Press, Limited, 2000.

Hunter, Charles T., SJ. "The Young Belizean Church: A Jesuit Mission Comes of Age." *Jesuit Bulletin*. Summer. 1983: 10-12.

Hunter, Yvonne, RSM. *The Sisters of Mercy in Belize, 1883–1983*. Cumberland, RI: Province of Providence Communications, Sisters of Mercy, 1984.

"*Independence*: Free but Vulnerable." *Time*. 5 Oct. 1981: 42.

Jennings, Nicola. "Service Trip to Belize, a stirring experience for Lexington teens." *Lexington Herald-Leader*. 5 Aug. 1998.

Lynn's Heart Newsletter. Prospect, KY. Nov. 1994. Nov. 1995.

Mahler, Richard and Steele Wotkyns. *Belize: A Natural Destination*. 3rd ed. Santa Fe: John Muir Publications, 1995.

Miller, Carlos Ledson. *Belize*. Xlibris Corporation, 1999.

Miller, Thomas. "Inside Chiquibul: Exploring Central America's Longest Cave," *National Geographic*. Apr. 2000: 54-71.

Mueller, Reuben H. "An Adventure in Ecumenical Cooperation." *The Documents of Vatican II*. New York: Guild Press, America Press, Association Press, 1966, xx-xxi.

Nolan, Mark. "Cover Quotation," *Cockscomb Basin Wildlife Sanctuary*. Caye Caulker, Belize: Producciones de la Hamaca and Gays Mills, Wisconsin, USA: Orang-utan Press, 1996.

Rabinowitz, Alan. Foreword. *Cockscomb Basin Wildlife Sanctuary*. Caye Caulker, Belize: Producciones de la Hamaca and Gays Mills, Wisconsin, USA: Orang-utan Press, 1996, xi.

Raley, Judy, SCN. "San Ignacio Parish Team Shares Its Talents." *Christian Herald* [Belize City] 18 Nov. 1979: 5.

Rochford, Thomas, SJ. *Jesuit Bulletin*. Fall 1988: 6.

"The Pastoral Constitution on the Church in the Modern World." *The Documents of Vatican II*. New York: Guild Press, American Press, Association Press, 1966, 238-318.

Rust, Susie Post. "The Garifuna: Weaving a Future from a Tangled Past." *National Geographic*. Sept. 2001: 102-113.

Saqui, Ernesto. "A History of Maya Center," *Cockscomb Basin Wildlife Sanctuary*. Caye Caulker, Belize: Producciones de la Hamaca and Gays Mills, Wisconsin, USA: Orang-utan Press, 1996, 25-27.

Schumacher, Ernst. *Small Is Beautiful*. New York: Harper and Row, 1973.

Shoman, Assad. *Thirteen Chapters of A History of Belize*. Belize City: The Angelus Press Limited, 1994.

SCNews. Mar. 1984: 4, 6.

SCN Mission News. Winter 1983: 7. Fall 1984: 4.

Villafane, Carol. "A Summer in Belize." *¡Adelante!* Fall/Winter 1999: 1-2.

INDEX